APPRECIATION FOR SULAK SIVARAKSA

HIS HOLINESS THE DALAI LAMA

Although material advances have contributed enormously to human welfare, they cannot create lasting happiness by themselves. I believe Sulak and I share a conviction that if we are to solve human problems, economic and technological development must be accompanied by an inner spiritual growth. And if we succeed in fulfilling both these goals, we will surely create a happier and more peaceful world.

AUNG SAN SUU KYI

Sulak, one of Asia's leading social thinkers, describes the "spirit of Buddhist development: as one where inner strength must be cultivated along with compassion and loving kindness." He sees the goals of Buddhist development as "equality, love, freedom, and liberation."

MAIREAD MAGUIRE

By the pivotal nature of his work, which bridges the artificial divides of North and South, Buddhist and non-Buddhist, self and other, bringing a healthy mix of universalism, and concern for local culture, and by the exemplary courage he has manifested in "speaking truth to power," Sulak Sivaraksa has made, and continues to make, a major contribution to peace and justice in his native Thailand, as well as in the world as a whole.

THICH NHAT HANH

Sulak offers a clear picture of what is going on, and he does so as a participant, not just as an observer. He is a teacher and an organizer, a *bodhisattva* who devotes all his energies to helping others.

JOANNA MACY

Sulak is one of the heroes of our time, offering us deep wisdom and refreshingly sane alternatives to the earth-destroying religions of consumerism, greed, and exploitation.

JACK KORNFIELD

Like Gandhi, Sulak offers great inspiration to a civilization that has lost its way.

STEPHEN BATCHELOR

An irrepressible campaigner for a sane and just society, Sulak unites the strengths of a traditional Dharmic sensibility with the critical rigor of a Western-educated intellectual. His life offers an heroic example of engaged Buddhism in practice.

JOHN B. COBB, JR.

In the entire world I know of no one who understands the situation more clearly and acts more effectively and consistently to bring the resources of a great religious tradition to bear on the critical issues of our time than Sulak Sivaraksa. I wish I could point to equally effective Christian leaders. I cannot. But perhaps we Christians can be inspired by him and learn from him, and can find the strength to act creatively.

WALDEN BELLO

With the crash of the economy, the question of alternatives to the current economic model has become extremely urgent. ... Sulak Sivaraksa has been in the forefront of developing a thoroughgoing critique of consumerism.

JOHN RALSTON SAUL

Whenever I ask myself a basic question of public ethics and public action, I end up wondering what Sulak would think. He has that great virtue of being true to himself and to the standards which somehow link all great moral philosophies. ... Sulak is an unstoppable force working on justice from a Buddhist point of view.

THE WISDOM OF SUSTAINABILITY

Buddhist Economics for the 21st Century

SULAK SIVARAKSA

Edited by Arnold Kotler and Nicholas Bennett

koa books

Kihei, Hawai'i

Koa Books
P.O. Box 822
Kihei, Hawai'i 96753
www.koabooks.com

Copyright © 2009 by Sulak Sivaraksa
Cover design by Lisa Carta
Book design by Silk Type
Printed in the United States of America
Distributed in North America by SCB Distributors, www.scbdistributors.com
Distributed in Asia by Silkworm Books, www..silkwormbooks.com
For more about this book and Sulak Sivaraksa's work, visit
www.wisdomofsustainability.com

Pubisher's Cataloging-in-Publication

Sulak Sivaraksa.

The wisdom of sustainability : Buddhist economics for the 21st
century / Sulak Sivaraksa ; edited by Arnold Kotler and Nicholas
Bennett. -- Kihei, Hawai'i : Koa Books ; Chiang Mai, Thailand :
Silkworm Books, c2009.
    p. ; cm.
    ISBN: 978- 0- 9821656- 1- 4
    1. Buddhism and social problems. 2. Economic development--
Religious aspects-- Buddhism. 3. Economics. 4. Sustainability--
Religious aspects-- Buddhism. I. Kotler, Arnold, 1946- II. Bennett,
Nicholas. III. Title. IV. Title: Buddhist economics for the 21st
century.

HN40.B8 S85 2009
294.3376--dc22   2009

1 2 3 4 5 6 7 8 9 / 13 12 11 10 09

CONTENTS

བཀའ་བློན་ཁྲི་པ་རམ་གདོང་སྒྲོལ་བཟང་བསྟན་འཛིན།

FOREWORD

All living creatures on earth are being threatened today by violence, terrorism, economic disparity, environmental degradation, and so-called religious intolerance or civilizational conflicts. All these problems are being created by human beings through the exploitation of negative emotions such as greed and hatred. Industrialization has enabled humanity to produce more commodities than people really need, which has necessitated the creation of markets and the exploitation of greed through indoctrination and brainwashing.

People are taught to compare and compete, so that ignorance and greed escalate endlessly, reducing individuals to consuming machines. We have lost the power of discernment and cannot differentiate between need and greed. Economic imperialists occupy the human mind, and human misery has been globalized. The disparity between unlimited desires and limited resources has not only made the economic infra-structure unsustainable but has also damaged our environment and ecosystems almost beyond repair. Gandhi's statement that "mother earth can well satisfy every living creature on it, but it can never satisfy even one person's greed," has proven true. As wealth has become the only value for far too many human beings, the principle of might makes right has become the order of the day—even more so than in primitive times. Human destiny seems almost hopeless.

In spite of this, Ajarn Sulak, a distinguished practitioner and engaged Buddhist, remains optimistic, continuing to make every effort to save the world based on the teachings of the Buddha. A sustainable economy based on right livelihood, peaceful societies through moral governance, and development from the bottom up (*Sarvodaya*) are some of the fundamental remedies and alternatives he proposes to reverse the present situation.

I greatly appreciate his right effort for putting his right view in this wonderful book, so that fellow human beings will come to share his right understanding. I trust this book will immensely benefit all its readers. *Sarvamangalam.*

Samdhong Rinpoche
Kalon Tripa (Prime Minister)
Tibetan Government-in-Exile
Dharamsala, India
February 20, 2009

DEDICATED TO

Maurice Anthony Ash (October 31, 1919 – January 27, 2003), an English buddhist philanthropist with a clear vision of truth, goodness, and beauty.

Lillian Willoughby (January 29, 1915 – January 15, 2009), an American Quaker who dedicated her life to fighting nonviolently for peace and justice, with a wonderful sense of humor.

THE WISDOM OF SUSTAINABILITY

INTRODUCTION

In the Thai language, *Ajarn* is an honorific term for someone you respect and have learned a great deal from. Ajarn Sulak and I have been friends and protagonists for more than thirty-five years. We met in 1972 when I was working in Bangkok and had invited Ivan Illich to meet with Thai intellectuals and student leaders. Already Sulak was editing the Social Science Review and mentoring a group of student leaders in nonviolent social action. We then became involved together in the tumultuous events in Thailand in 1973, 1976, and beyond.

After the bloody military coup of October 1976, when thousands of students fled the cities to join the Communist Party of Thailand in the jungles in the north and south of the country, and thousands of others were arrested, together we created the first human rights organization in Thailand out of the Coordinating Group for Religion in Society. Over a three-year period, we managed to get more than 11,000 people out of prison. During part of this time, Sulak had to retreat in the first of his several exiles; in fact, he spent his first night of exile in my parents' house in London. On his return some months later and during much of the 1980s, he did more than anyone else to heal the huge rifts in Thai society and arrange for returning student leaders to be reintegrated into society.

He was already, at that time, an activist Buddhist practitioner and a Siamese nationalist and royalist, positions he has maintained ever since. He established a publishing house and bookshop that became the main meeting place for Bangkok intellectuals, and arranged for Thich Nhat Hanh to visit and participate in a training program in nonviolent action for young activists.

Ajarn Sulak has always been surrounded by young men and women who want to play a role in a more human-centered development process. When he realized that many of them were getting burned out in their struggles, he managed to secure donations of money and land and built an ashram outside of Bangkok where activists can retreat and recharge their batteries in peace and tranquility, following basic Buddhist wisdom and meditation practices.

I left Bangkok in 1979 and spent the next twenty-five years working for the United Nations and the World Bank throughout the world. During this period Sulak and my paths crossed in Bangkok and elsewhere. In Japan in 1992, for example, we continued our discussions of the role that Buddhism might play in the future development of his country. I was therefore not surprised when he asked me to help edit his talks and articles into this book on Buddhist economics and sustainability.

Sulak's understanding of the message of the Buddha—starting with the simple practices of breathing and meditation—permeates every page of this book, as does his belief that nonviolence (*ahimsa*) is the central tenet of Buddhism. It is clear to Sulak that the world is sick and that action needs to be taken to heal it now, before it is too late. Peace needs to replace war, nonviolence to replace violence, generosity to replace greed, love to replace hatred, and understanding to replace ignorance. We must learn to love our environment and stop trying to conquer it. Today in much of Asia, Buddhism has to compete with the new religion of consumerism. According to Sulak, there are now more prostitutes than monks in his country, and shopping malls have replaced temples as centers of community activity. Only in places where consumerism and globalization have not spread their tentacles, such as Bhutan and amongst Tibetan exiles, are traditional Buddhist practices still thriving at the grassroots level. The challenge that Sulak and other engaged Buddhists face is how to show that Buddhism can be a force to soften the damage caused to the human spirit by the onward march of globalization.

Sulak quite rightly attacks the neoliberal agenda of the World Bank (where I used to work) and the unproven hypothesis that if the Gross Domestic Product (GDP) increases in a particular society, the citizens will automatically be better off. Man cannot live by bread alone. Once our basic needs for food, shelter, clothing, and health are met, our needs for security, peace, and spirituality must also be addressed. These are harder to identify and much harder to operationalize. In *The Wisdom of Sustainability,* Sulak explores replacing GDP with the still imprecise but important concept of Gross National Happiness (GNH). According to Western development specialists, we can increase happiness and satisfaction by increasing our consumption of goods and services; whilst according to Buddhists, our happiness and satisfaction can only be increased by reducing our desire for things.

In this important new book, Ajarn Sulak shines light on globalization, development, violence, and governance from a Buddhist perspective. Known as a gadfly throughout Asia, Sulak challenges the status quo on a daily basis, and, even as I write, he has once again been accused of *lèse majesté* (treason against a member of the Thai royal family), a serious offense. Still, he continues without fear criticizing members of the royal family, prime ministers, army generals, and other powers that be, and this fearlessness allows his writings to be so fresh and pointed.

Sulak has always been surrounded by good friends, which, according to the Buddha, is essential if we want to achieve anything in this life. He has helped many young people take their first steps toward a spiritually based social activism, and continues to provide them with moral support as they branch off in their own directions. There is hardly a non-governmental organization that does not have someone on its staff whom Sulak has helped. Although many of his friends are in Thailand, more aptly called Siam, others can be found throughout the world, on virtually every continent. Now in his mid-seventies, Sulak still travels the world to teach and visit his wide network of friends.

Our world is being ripped apart by conflict, as the rich get richer and the poor live off their crumbs, hundreds are killed and maimed every day in Africa and the Middle East, and many thousands more starve to death. Our world needs to be healed—everywhere, at every level. We know what to do, but as flawed individuals, it is sometimes difficult to succeed. According to Ajarn Sulak, we need to start the healing at the individual level, and only then can we make our planet a more habitable place. The wisdom of sustainability Sulak talks about is on both individual and global levels. This book provides a map of where we could be going. It is our hope and our challenge.

Nicholas Bennett, Coeditor
Phuket, Thailand
February 2009

1

—

Heavenly Messengers

When Prince Siddhartha—the future Buddha—left his palace at the age of twenty-nine, he encountered for the first time a sick man, an elderly man, a corpse, and a wandering monk. Despairing, he left the comforts of home and entered the holy life, determined to overcome suffering and death. Some time later, he realized that these four sights had been heavenly messengers.

I met James Wolfensohn, president of the World Bank, in 1998, and he asked about Asia's recent economic collapse that had begun in my country.* I told him I thought it had been a heavenly messenger to encourage us to seek alternatives to economic globalization.

In the years following World War II, governments and individuals around the world worked enthusiastically together to try to build a better world. They established the United Nations as the first truly universal forum where small, poor countries could rub shoulders with powerful,

---

*My country was known as Siam until 1939, when its name was changed to Thailand, a hybrid Anglicized word emblematic of the crisis of traditional Siamese Buddhist values. I generally refer to the country as Siam, not Thailand.

rich ones on matters of common concern, on the basis of equality. They created the World Bank and the International Monetary Fund—the Bretton Woods institutions—to generate prosperity for all. The World Bank's mission, engraved on the walls of its Washington, D.C., headquarters, is to eradicate poverty.

The Bank's strategy for creating wealth has been to impose deregulation, privatization, and structural adjustment on the economies of nations. Deregulation is the removal of government restrictions on business. Privatization is the transfer of ownership from the public to the private sector. Structural adjustments are requirements imposed, usually on third-world countries, in order to receive loans from the World Bank or similar lenders. These adjustments—often deregulation and privatization—are intended to generate wealth. Although the Bretton Woods' founders were sincere in their efforts to bring an end to poverty, in fact the institutions and instruments they created have brought about increased inequality in wealth, as well as environmental degradation and cultural deterioration. Using the World Bank's own definition of poverty, the number of poor people has increased.

Mr. Wolfensohn asked me to say more, and I told him that globalization—which really should be called free-market fundamentalism—is a demonic religion imposing materialistic values on developing as well as industrialized nations, driving individuals to try to earn more to acquire more in a never-ending cycle of greed and insecurity. The World Bank and other Bretton Woods institutions presume the superiority of industrialization, the monetary economy, and modernity over agrarian lifestyles, subsistence economies, and indigeneity, making globalization a new form of colonialism. The term *modernization* is, in fact, racially coded; its precursor was *Europeanization*.

Capitalism's promise to bring about emancipation through perpetual economic growth is, to use Jerry Mander's word, insane. Nothing can grow forever. There are limits. Before we irretrievably erode the matter of our mother earth, we need to change direction and build a future based on wisdom and compassion. There are simply not enough resources for everyone to live a first-world lifestyle.

Buddhadasa Bhikkhu, my spiritual teacher, emphasized the importance of staying close to nature. He would look at the banyan tree in front of his hut and point to the plants and animals living peacefully in its shade. The first law of the natural world, he said, is interdependence.

When we are in harmony with nature, we feel nurtured and profoundly content. The Buddha called this *Dharma*, the natural order of things. Dharma emphasizes sentience—the alive-nature of phenomena, including our mind. As we come to understand natural Dharma, we also discover our own potential and responsibilities. At the core of Dharma is the spirit of free inquiry. After six years of intense effort, Prince Siddhartha overcame his attachment to greed, hatred, and ignorance, and became a Buddha, "an awakened one." He shared his insight with fellow yogis, and this event is known as "turning the Wheel of the Dharma."

❖ ❖ ❖

Globalization sounds value-neutral. It preaches the interdependence of nations, the mutuality of their interests, and the shared benefits of their exchanges. But during the half-century of globalization's ascendance on the world stage, inequities between haves and have-nots—North and South, investors and workers, agribusiness and peasants—have increased exponentially, triggering the near-total dependence of so-called developing countries on developed ones. As a result of this free-market fundamentalism, environments have been destroyed and economies have collapsed.

Even in the midst of a global economic meltdown, neoliberal ideologues continue to push to remove trade barriers and restructure economies. Their faith in the emancipatory power of the free market must be based on unmitigated greed. These are intelligent individuals; they cannot be this blind or naïve. Neoliberals regard modernity as is its own justification, and permit it to devour all other social and cultural beliefs and aspirations. We need to intensify our criticism and redefine globalization's contours and content.

In Siam, consumer culture, through the mass media, has replaced Buddhist virtues. To overcome these false values promoted in the name of economic development, we need to return to our spiritual roots.

❖ ❖ ❖

A monk asked the Buddha, "I have been meditating for many years to be able to walk on water."

The Buddha replied, "It would be better to hire a boatman."

Another religious leader asked the Buddha, "What practices do your monks follow?"

The Buddha answered, "They walk, stand, lie down, sit, eat, and drink."

"What is special about that?" the man asked.

The Buddha explained, "While walking, they know that they are walking. When standing, they know that they are standing. When lying down, they know that they are lying down. ..."

As Thich Nhat Hanh says, the miracle is to walk on the earth mindfully, to touch the depth and sacred presence of each moment. Meditation helps us see the traits that dominate our consciousness—hatred *and* love, ignorance *and* wisdom, fear *and* courage. When we acknowledge the full range of qualities within us, our ignorance begins to fade, and wisdom and compassion arise naturally. The practice of mindful breathing restructures our consciousness and helps us develop critical self-awareness. We become more able to see the structural violence in ourselves and the world.

❖ ❖ ❖

Structural violence is a term coined in the 1960s by Johan Galtung, the founder of peace studies as an academic discipline. It refers to systematic ways a society's resources are distributed unequally and unfairly, preventing people from meeting their basic needs. Structural violence includes elitism, ethnocentrism, classism, racism, sexism, nationalism, heterosexism, and ageism.

Structural violence may be political, repressive, economic, or exploitative. Unequal access to resources, power, education, health care, or legal standing are forms of structural violence. When inner-city children attend inadequate schools while others do not, when laborers work in inhumane conditions, structural violence exists.

Social structures are not permanent or natural phenomena. They evolve—through political and historical developments—and usually refer to organizations, institutions, laws, and ideologies. Social structures influence action by creating frameworks of propriety that govern those within the structures.

Social structures pressure us to adopt desired dogma, establishing what is then regarded as normative. Each structure creates boundaries to what is acceptable, speakable, and thinkable. These boundaries define "the truth." They describe our worldview, and we accept it without question. We become spectators, even cheerleaders. When our mind gives rise to an idea that is "outside the box," we feel too afraid to seek the truth.

The power of social structures is enormous. They influence our thoughts, actions, attitudes, desires, and even our bodies. When we accept this canon, we enjoy a privileged status. When we challenge or reject it, we become marginalized. We have to see the relationships between social structures, self-surveillance, and self-censorship. To enforce social constructions, institutions intimidate us. Modern medicine fills us with the fear of illness, aging, and even ugliness. Religions might deceive us; Buddhist temples in my country have become terribly rich from donations people make in order to gain merit and thus ensure for themselves an auspicious rebirth. Governments control us through fear: fear of jail or even execution.

"National security," "private property," and "free-market capitalism" are social structures. By showcasing these and other structures, our education system teaches students to be subservient to power and accept the status quo rather than work to overturn injustice. The central operating concept of the global economy is "private property." The West invented this, and we Asians dutifully have followed their lead. Recently the government in India declared that (literally) every drop of rain in Rajasthan belongs to them, and they will, in turn, provide concessions to private companies to buy and sell this rainwater.

The media—almost all are for-profit corporations—are expert in legitimizing the actions of those in power. It is essential that we learn to analyze structural violence and social structures. In this age of extreme modernism, a time of terror, we need to understand how our systems of thought have been crafted, so when a heavenly messenger awakens us, we will know what is true.

2

—

CREATING A CULTURE OF PEACE

Following the September 11, 2001, terrorist attacks on the World Trade
Center, His Holiness the Dalai Lama offered these words to then-
President George W. Bush: "We need to think seriously whether a violent action is the right thing to do and in the greater interest of the
nation and people in the long run. I believe violence will only increase
the cycle of violence."

President Bush responded by attacking Afghanistan and, less than
eighteen months later, Iraq. He said his country's mission was "to rid the
world of evil," emphasizing a "crusade" against the "Axis of Evil"—Iraq,
Iran, and North Korea. I cringed when I heard his words, remembering
that Hitler and Stalin also wanted to rid the world of evil.

The great Russian author Alexander Solzhenitsyn wrote:

> If only it were all so simple! If only there were evil people somewhere,
> insidiously committing evil deeds, and it were necessary only to separate
> them from the rest of us and destroy them. But the line dividing good

and evil cuts through the heart of every human being, and who is willing to destroy a piece of his own heart?

Conflicts flare up over neighbors' fences and national borders, while cleaning the kitchen or cleaning up the environment. They involve our most intimate relationships or encounters with strangers. Conflicts are inevitable. Grappling with conflict provides the opportunity for knowledge, healing, and growth.

First, we need to stop simply blaming the other party and identify where our own rigid and self-righteous views make their claim on us. At the same time, we must allow in others' viewpoints. When we have explored our own position thoroughly, it is easier to understand those with whom we are in conflict.

Visualize the person you despise the most. Contemplate his or her features that make you most angry. Then think about what makes him happy and what makes him suffer. What motivates his actions? Try to see patterns. Meditating this way, compassion and insight will arise in your heart, like fresh water filling a spring. You may need to repeat the exercise many times before you have this experience. Eventually your anger will vanish. Next, do the same exercise on yourself—to understand your own greed, hatred, and ignorance. With a deeper understanding of yourself, you will see similarities with others. This is essential for preventing and resolving conflicts.

When attacked, your choice isn't simply between violence and inaction. Other responses, including dialogue, law enforcement, negotiation, and diplomacy, are possible. When parties take the time to listen to each other, animosity often dissolves. Rather than divide the world into good and evil, we need to see others, first and foremost, as our fellow human beings.

When asked to summarize the Buddha's teachings, third-century philosopher Nagarjuna answered in one word: ahimsa, nonviolence. Nonviolence does not mean doing nothing. It is a proactive, comprehensive process of addressing conflicts through communication and resource sharing. According to the Buddha, every act of violence is preceded by an intention, conscious or unconscious. To create a culture of peace, we must begin by acknowledging the violence in our own hearts and then learn to disarm it. Greed, hatred, or ignorance is at the core of every violent action. Wisdom and compassion are at the base of every act of nonviolence.

Every one of our actions has an effect. In the *Dhammapada*, the Buddha teaches, "Hatred does not eradicate hatred. Only by loving kindness is hatred dissolved. This law is ancient and eternal." Gandhi summarized it well: "An eye for an eye just makes the whole world blind." The Buddha also said, "If you act with a corrupt mind, suffering will follow. … If you act with a peaceful mind, peace will follow." We cannot avoid the results of our *karma*. We must be mindful of each act of our lives. Violence is not the result of a faulty political economy. Violence springs from human consciousness.

A culture of violence is one that produces, normalizes, and consumes ideas of division and hatred. Modern societies invest massively in war and violence. The U.S. spends nearly half of the world's total, followed distantly by the UK, France, Japan, and China. Almost every third-world country also invests far too much in its own military budget, and many also host U.S. bases on their territory.

Martin Luther King, Jr., observed that "our scientific power has outrun our spiritual power. We have guided missiles and misguided men." Gandhi noted, "We are constantly being astonished at the amazing discoveries in the field of violence. But I maintain that far more undreamt of and seemingly impossible discoveries will be made in the field of nonviolence." We live in an age of both pluralism and terror, and it is critical for us to articulate what might constitute a culture of peace. Nonviolence is Buddhism's master precept.

Peacekeeping, peacemaking, and peacebuilding are three responses to conflict. Peacekeeping stops people from attacking each other. This minimizes the damage but does not ensure stability. We need to put out the fires, but it would be better to prevent them in the first place by addressing the underlying causes.

Peacekeeping sometimes employs the means of conflict to end conflict. At other times, small numbers of people have been able to penetrate violent situations by practicing nonviolence. When the Nazis tried to exterminate the Jews of Denmark, King Fredrick IX declared that if his Jewish subjects were captured, he, too, would wear the Star of David and be subject to arrest. As a result, the Germans did not touch the Danish Jews. Badshah Khan, a devout Muslim, known as the Gandhi of the Pakistan-Afghanistan frontier, was able to persuade his Pashtun brothers to renounce arms and join him in a 100,000-man army of nonviolence.

The 1973 overthrow of the Thai dictatorship, the end of the Marcos government in the Philippines, and the collapse of communism in Eastern Europe are all examples of the use of nonviolence to end violence and oppression and bring about lasting social change. The images of a lone protestor standing in front of a tank in Tiananmen Square and Daw Aung San Suu Kyi confronting the Burmese military are reminders of the great moral and physical courage it takes to engage in nonviolence.

The paradigm articulated by President Bush needs to be dismantled. The true power of America is not its wealth or military might, but its ideals of liberty, democracy, and generosity. We must stop investing in war and violence, and invest instead in peace and nonviolence. Dennis Kucinich has introduced a resolution in the U.S. Congress to create a cabinet-level Department of Peace.

The second response to conflict—peacemaking—involves not just intervening, but actually settling conflicts. The most important element of peacemaking is dialogue. What we call dialogue is often just two monologues. Genuine dialogue requires active listening. We need to abandon our idea of a particular outcome and remain quiet within. When both sides feel heard, creative problem solving can bring unanticipated results. Reconciliation is key. Acknowledging the past alleviates suffering, heals injustice, and fosters transformation. Called *restorative justice*, victim and perpetrator listen to each other deeply—difficult as that may be—and, as a result, both change. This kind of education, rather than punishment, minimizes recidivism.

Peacebuilding, the third response, is the never-ending effort to create a peaceful society. It begins at the grassroots level and includes a wide range of long-term solutions—education, grassroots democracy, land reform, poverty alleviation. Like the little parrot in the *Jataka* tale of the Buddha's former life, a peacebuilder mobilizes his community to bring water drop by drop to quench the raging fire. Peacebuilding must be based on nonviolence, which, in turn, must be based on wisdom and compassion. These kinds of activities garner few headlines but are the most meaningful responses to conflict. Once a war has started, it is nearly impossible to stop. We need to stop the next war now by creating just and truly democratic societies.

When the Buddha came to understand how suffering arises, he was able to transform the processes that cause and sustain it. He described this insight using the language of four noble truths:

1. Suffering exists.
2. Suffering has causes.
3. We can stop producing the causes of suffering.
4. A path of mindful living can show us the way.

Let us apply these four truths to situations of conflict. We begin by acknowledging both sides' suffering. Each adversary states his experience clearly, with witnesses present to acknowledge their statements. This is the first noble truth, the acknowledgment of suffering.

Second, we try to understand the external *and* psychological roots of the conflict. When we project our emotions onto an object (animate or inanimate), we experience the "other" as having traits which, in fact, dwell first in our own unconscious mind. We fail to see the line between the object and our own feelings. To discover the roots of any conflict, we must also examine its psychological dimensions. With this understanding, we can explore the external conditions more clearly.

The third noble truth is the cessation of the causes of suffering. This does not presuppose that we can reach a state that is conflict-free, but encourages us to grapple with the details—internal and external—every time. Conflict can be an opportunity to go directly to the heart of the matter and learn more about ourselves.

The fourth noble truth—peace as a way of life—shows us how to live in ways that reduce suffering and conflict. The Buddha called this the eightfold path:

1. Right Understanding: understanding the four noble truths.
2. Right Thought: freedom from that which cannot bring satisfaction.
3. Right Speech: speaking truthfully and skillfully.
4. Right Action: not killing, stealing, or indulging in irresponsible sexual behavior.
5. Right Livelihood: not engaging in a profession that brings harm to others.
6. Right Effort: encouraging wholesome states of mind.
7. Right Mindfulness: awareness of the physical and mental dimensions of our experience.
8. Right Concentration: staying focused.

This eightfold path encourages peacebuilding as a way of life. It points to ways that awareness can be deepened and the parts of our lives brought into harmony. We begin by living mindfully. Then we can use these tools to dismantle oppressive systems and create a culture of peace.

3

—

Development from the Bottom Up

There is an old Thai saying, "In the fields there is rice; in the water there are fish." Before colonialism, the fertile lands of Southeast Asia—known as the Rice Bowl of Asia—provided food for all its people. Plants grew everywhere, wildlife was plentiful, jungles produced teak and other hardwoods, and the human population was sparse. Communities farmed their own land, wove their own cloth, and were governed and protected by their own institutions—family, community, and a highly developed system of seniority. Production was cooperative and geared toward self-sufficiency and maintaining the balance of nature.

Today 60 percent of the children in rural Siam suffer from malnutrition, millions of Indonesian peasants migrate to the slums of Jakarta, thousands of Filipino farmers have left their land to find work in the Middle East and elsewhere, and small fishermen on the Malaysian coast are barely surviving. Colonization by Western powers caused an upheaval in formerly self-sustaining village production systems. When foreign companies took over large tracts of land for rubber, sugar cane, coconut, and banana plantations, the cash economy replaced barter, and farming for export shifted control of villagers' destinies from within their own communities to distant market forces. Small farms were acquired by local elites, and new classes of tenant farmers, sharecroppers, and farmworkers emerged. For more than half a century, colonialism has been replaced by neocolonialism. Countries that appear to be independent are, in fact, under such enormous economic pressure from the West, they are as-though still colonized. Rural development policies by aid organizations concentrate on agribusiness, forcing peasants to depend on the marketplace for clothing, electricity, water, fuel, construction materials, fertilizers, pesticides, livestock, and agricultural tools. Modernization has brought about more efficient production and an increase in the *average* standard of living, but the plight of individual peasants has worsened. Benefits have gone to exporters, landlords, plantation owners, mill owners, large farmers, professionals, and high-ranking government officials. This growth of an elite class has led to an increased demand for consumer goods, which, in turn, requires increased agricultural exports.

With their near-total dependence on market forces, the underclasses are finding it difficult to purchase enough food to eat. They sell their produce at market prices; pay off their debts for fertilizer, pesticides, and the other items they use in production; and often don't have enough cash or produce for themselves. When there is a drought or flooding, the problems multiply.

It is the wealthy farmers with enough land to produce a surplus— a small minority of the rural population—who qualify for bank loans to modernize their production and benefit from government-support schemes. Agribusinesses are flourishing, extending their operations to more and more remote areas. They run their farms and plantations with the labor of farmworkers, who receive subsistence wages, or tenant farmers, for whom they supply raw materials and technology in exchange for up to half the produce.

Farmworkers and sharecroppers have no bargaining power over market prices, rents, and daily wages. Organizing has not helped. Agricultural cooperatives and farmers' unions are tightly controlled by governments that serve the interests of wealthy farmers. When governments form organizations like the Association of Southeast Asian Nations, they simply share methods of repression. For the tenant farmers, production costs increase more quickly than income and they go to moneylenders, who charge them exorbitant interest. Plagued by mounting debts, they need supplemental sources of income, and millions flock to the cities to do heavy labor for low wages.

Young girls work as servants or unskilled factory workers, or are forced into prostitution. The Southeast Asian sex market is thriving. Women are also "exported" to Europe, Hong Kong, and Japan. Children work illegally in sweatshops under harsh conditions. Some are even sold abroad. This massive urban migration has done little to solve the problems of those who migrate or those left at home. Few of the new city dwellers are able to send money back to their families. Some resort to crime.

Modernized agriculture also brings large-scale depletion of natural resources. Forests are rapidly disappearing, and with them much wildlife. The mudfish and edible frogs that thrived in the rice fields and provided a rich source of food for the peasants are being killed by insecticides. Large-scale trawler fishing is depleting marine life and destroying the livelihoods of small fishermen.

When power is centralized, individuals lose control over their destinies. Community values are rarely honored when remote institutions govern their lives. Former Czech President Vaclav Havel stated:

> Enormous private multinational corporations are curiously like socialist states, with industrialization, centralization, specialization, monopolization. Finally with automation and computerization, the elements of depersonalization and the loss of meaning in work become more and more profound everywhere. Along with that goes the general manipulation of people's lives by the system (no matter how inconspicuous such manipulation may be), comparable with that of the totalitarian state.

In the free-trade model of development, multinational corporations replace the village or community as the matrix for human interaction. The argument for free trade is predicated on the theory of comparative advantage brought forth in the nineteenth century by David Ricardo. According to this theory, free trade encourages each country to pursue the economic activities for which it is best suited, thereby promoting comparative advantage and economic efficiency for all. Significant considerations are, however, overlooked. Free-trade advocates do not concern themselves with which groups in society prosper and which ones fall behind. And the effects of trade on non-economic values are not addressed, because so-called developed societies see everything through the lens of economics, and then they transmit that hyper-materialist view into a global perspective. Governments become like machines to maximize opportunities for capitalist investors.

We need to find ways to make communities stronger—socially, politically, and economically. We need to reestablish the commons—the public sphere. We need to engage community members to participate in making decisions about the things that affect their lives and livelihoods. And we need to address the dilemmas caused by the increased dependence of third-world economies on international trade.

Corporations move their production facilities to the country that allows the greatest exploitation of workers and the least protection of the environment. Reduced wages and erosion of workers' rights are the cornerstones of the economic policies of countries that compete for the comparative advantage of having cheap labor. We are told that protecting workers' rights will be self-defeating, as it will cause employers to relocate to less conscientious countries. Nations and corporations, and the recent merger of the two, are often perpetrators of structural violence. Their policies increase disparities in wealth, deplete natural resources, and alienate individuals from their root cultures. Driven by profit, these policies seem indifferent to people's discontent.

As a Buddhist, I do not consider the exploitation of comparative advantage to be the ultimate objective of society. I am interested in a social organization's capacity to address human suffering, promote justice, and allow individuals to realize their potential. I have seen the effects of free trade on my country, where farmers have been persuaded to abandon self-sufficiency and instead, grow crops for export. These small farmers are then unable to compete with the large, highly efficient farms and, as a consequence, lose their land, forcing them to seek employment in urban construction or manufacturing for $5 a day or less, while their daughters might be lured into prostitution. Outcomes like these, amazingly, constitute "success" for the economic planners who record only the increase in GDP and ignore social disarray and environmental devastation.

Environmental protection must be regulated by international organizations. When individual countries enforce measures to protect the environment, multinational corporations simply migrate to less restrictive places. Countries need protection from having to sacrifice their environments to attract business. We need economies that promote human values, seek to limit suffering, and are committed to democratic principles, rather than ones dependent on global trade and a blind commitment to neoliberal economic policies.

We must stop exploiting the earth and her people and rebuild our economies on the basis of wisdom and compassion. This is what E. F. Schumacher called Buddhist economics—societies where people help each other in difficult times, where power is shared rather than fought over, where nature is respected and wisdom cherished. It took a British Catholic, E. F. Schumacher, to remind us that Buddhist economics could serve as an example for those who regard human beings more highly than money. Buddhist economics must be based on sustainability, not unlimited growth. Today, there are good people everywhere taking concrete steps to manifest this vision, with a strong determination to end oppression and move societies in the direction of sustainability.

❖❖❖

The people of my country, although never colonized politically, were colonized intellectually and thus alienated from our Buddhist roots. The Buddhist Kingdom of Siam now has more prostitutes than monks. Peasant farmers have migrated to urban slums or remain laborers on land they used to own. Bangkok, once a beautiful city, is now polluted and ugly.

Capitalism brainwashes us through advertising and the skewing of priorities to think we need to become someone other than ourselves to have value. But we can never become more than ourselves by rejecting who we are. When we are firmly rooted in self-respect, we can make healthy choices. In rural Thai society, the people believe that everyone has Buddha nature, the potential to attain deep understanding. From this viewpoint, the poor and marginalized are entitled to the same degree of dignity as you and I. The localization of power and economy can be the basis for spiritual health and well-being.

Grassroots activists in Siam have begun farming in traditional ways, forming cooperatives and creating a self-reliant economy. Many cultivate their crops without chemical fertilizers, and operate rice and buffalo banks, thus avoiding the moneylenders. A half-million people organized an Assembly of the Poor and staged nonviolent protests over a period of three months that forced the prime minister to give them rights they'd been denied for decades. Development from the bottom up emphasizes individual freedom and responsibility.

True development must be in harmony with the needs of people and the rhythms of the natural world. Humans are a part of the universe, not its masters. This awareness of the interrelatedness of all beings, as expressed in Buddhism, is lived in the traditions of indigenous peoples throughout the world. They do not separate the political from the personal or spiritual, but dwell in awareness of the sacredness of all life. This understanding guides their every step and every choice.

Cherokee medicine woman and Tibetan Buddhist teacher Dhyani Ywahoo says,

> There is a stream of compassionate wisdom of which we are all a part. From that flowing heart comes a great wisdom to which each of us is attuned. Peace is alive in us as a seed, as a song. To call it forth is a practice of clear vision and clear speech. See the beauty and praise the beauty, and wisdom's stream will flow abundantly in our heart.

For corporations, natural resources are just a source of economic benefit. When one location is exhausted, they move to the next. People are relevant only to the extent that they generate profits as laborers or consumers. The modern structural worldview has brought prosperity, democracy, and mobility to a few, and increased poverty to the world's majority, while reinforcing cronyism disguised as representative democracy.

Under this model of development, it is not unusual for citizens to be cut off from their roots. When the combine harvester was introduced in the rural, agriculture-based region around Lake Songkla in southern Siam, people's songs, dances, communal meals, and sense of home were replaced by a quick payment to the stranger for the rent of this machine. Today, it is hard to find a single farmer in the region who does not use this grinding behemoth to harvest his rice. Harvesting is quicker, but when they did it by hand, families relied on one another for help, and the work provided a cohesion to village life. Now, working-age men and women from Lake Songkla take jobs in nearby cities, leaving only the very young and very old at home in the villages. When whole families migrate to urban areas for low-paying jobs, they tend to live in unhealthy, dangerous places and require government services for basic needs they used to provide for themselves, further deteriorating their spirit and culture. Considerations like these remain outside the World Bank's lending decisions, leaving isolation and separation in their wake.

The developing world is constantly reminded by donor agencies to reevaluate their economic systems toward greater structural openness. We need to remind these agencies to reevaluate their *own* openness to re-envisioning the development process. Policy planning and evaluation based purely on quantitative analysis, such as doctors per thousand people or GDP per capita, do not address the wide range of human concerns. We need to find a common language between donor agencies and recipients that respects cultural identity and social diversity. The World Bank sees structural adjustment as the freeing up of markets. Local people experience it as cultural clear-cutting.

The word *development* is widely used but little understood. It is usually regarded as positive, like the words *liberty, freedom,* and *democracy.* Dr. Puey Ungphakorn, who played a central role in shaping Siam's economic development, enunciated eight prerequisites for development: liberty, peace, justice, mutual caring, worthy goals, well-planned procedures, efficiency, and the careful use of power properly checked. Dr. Puey cited increased income, improved health standards, economic stability, and distribution of the fruits of production throughout the nation as worthy development goals, as opposed to simply increasing the average per capita GDP. He cautioned against the view that national development is just a matter of economics and public welfare. Development has to do with all branches of knowledge and must be based on ethical principles.

Buddhadasa Bhikkhu pointed out that root meaning of the Thai word for development, *patana,* is "disorderliness," and a related Buddhist term, *vadhana,* can mean either "progress" or "regress." Ivan Illich pointed out that the Latin word *progressio,* a root idea in development, can mean "madness." It is difficult to contradict what Buddhadasa and Illich imply.

Different people use the word *development* differently. We must ask ourselves, what end result are we aiming toward? If our goal is to produce electricity, a clean public water supply, irrigation, and to aid the fishing and agricultural industries, we might decide to build a dam. But if our goal is the well-being of the citizenry, building a dam becomes questionable. How will the fruits of our development projects contribute toward making people more truly human, enhance relations among people, and encourage self-knowledge and insight into the nature of life?

Development can emphasize quantity or quality. With the former, we can measure results, but it is presumptuous to assume that more factories, schools, hospitals, food clothing, jobs, or income will necessarily enhance the quality of life. Although these are all necessary, they are not sufficient. People want and need to go further and search out and realize their fullest potential. This addresses the question of who are we, and that has to do with sacredness. Development must also take into account the essence of our humanity.

Looking at Gandhi's approach to life and his encounters with the West can serve us well here. "Gandhian Development," as I call it, is based on the same foundations as Buddhist philosophy, for it aims at the reduction of craving, avoidance of violence, and development of the spirit. This kind of true development is in accord with nature and the movements and rhythm of life. For Gandhi, quality of life was both the means and the end of development. He rejected both the production and accumulation of material things as life's aim, emphasizing instead the importance of spirit. He said the less we are dependent on material goods, the greater our freedom of spirit.

If we emphasize simple satisfactions, the preservation of traditional values, and gradual progress in matters both physical and spiritual, other values will follow. This helps develop independence and inter-dependence, rather than dependence on outside experts. At the village and national levels, Gandhian Development begins and ends with people who are in a strong position to be moral and courageous in their decision-making.

Some argue that adopting Gandhi's anti-material bias makes it impossible for development to attain its goals, but they forget that the bigger anything becomes, the more dehumanizing it becomes, espe-cially in the areas of machinery and administrative systems. We would do well to consider the words of E. F. Schumacher, who wrote, "The keynote to Buddhist economics is simplicity and nonviolence. From the economist's point of view, the marvel of the Buddhist way of life is the utter rationality of its pattern—amazingly small means leading to extraordinarily satisfactory results." Schumacher may be the first West-ern economist to emphasize that if the small can be made beautiful, economics can hold people as more important than production.

To economists who judge results by quantity, Gandhi's methods look counterproductive. When Schumacher began to study Gandhian meth-ods, he pointed out that it was probably a good thing that Gandhi did not understand the intricacies of economics, for it enabled his own genius and his emphasis on the spirit to shine through.

Gandhi's method begins at the village level, preserves village culture, and promotes progress in village life by increasing the type of production that does not require machinery. It makes play a part of life and work a part of play. The more self-sufficient villages are, the more village participation will be required in making decisions on the national level. This is true decentralization-of-power economics, both politically and culturally. To be sure, this will mean that industry will develop in the cities more slowly, but it offers no opportunity for cities to take advantage of rural areas, and rural people will be less inclined to stream to the cities if village life is satisfying and sustaining.

Using indigenous models like Buddhism is culturally appropriate for development in Asia. In Buddhist development, inner strength must be cultivated first, then compassion and loving kindness toward others. Work is not to "get ahead," but to enjoy working in harmony for basic needs, with others. A simple life can be satisfying without being exploitative. The Dharma emphasizes personal development that can heal individuals and, by doing so, help transform society.

What if agencies offered development aid in terms similar to the ways an aspirant follows a spiritual path—balancing head and heart, independence and interdependence, quantity and quality? A spiritual teacher does not solve a student's problems but empowers her to find answers on her own. When loans are designed to increase material prosperity, they cannot solve a society's problems.

Making sure that everyone has adequate food, clothing, shelter, and medicine is the starting point. These necessities are the foundation for building a spiritual ecology that emphasizes the simple, direct, and affordable satisfaction of needs, and not luxuries. When we feel nurtured by society and nature, we can envision a kind of development that focuses on individual *and* community capacity-building. The nongovernmental organization (NGO) movement—particularly the movement of *local* NGOs, directly accountable to local people rather than to international donors—has had a positive effect in this regard by affirming community values.

The Buddhist symbol of Indra's Net—a web with a mirror at each node reflecting all the other mirrors—can help us understand this development model. Each node encompasses the whole, and vice versa. Envision a community in which power is not just centralized but also exists in every corner. Individuals and communities determine their own direction and then ask for structural support. World Bank initiatives presently disregard the need for individuals to participate in the development process on their own terms. In this model, connections between groups and individuals are vital, as are cooperation and the democratic and dynamic interplay of all community sectors. This model contains clear, efficient decision-making methods, de-emphasizing the structural hierarchies of the institutions with whom development agencies usually partner.

The World Bank and other lending and donor agencies have expertise in infrastructural development and developing loans. It is unrealistic that suddenly they will take on issues of personal transformation, nor is it in anyone's interest that they do so. But we *do* need to cultivate connection and cooperation, and the World Bank could help by fostering just relations among sectors of developing societies.

For poverty to be lessened, space must be created for the poor to articulate their own visions. The notion of *expert* must be expanded beyond just those with Ph.D.s and abstract specialized knowledge to include those with hands-on experience and an integrated understanding. This participatory model of development is a small, yet positive step, toward creating a world in which interdependence is honored and organizations cultivate within themselves a kind of "social biodiversity."

We must challenge economic policies that are not accountable to the people they supposedly serve and challenge legal and judicial systems that maintain an unjust status quo. We need alternative economic and political strategies, as E. F. Schumacher said, "as if people mattered." We need education that encourages the integration of the many aspects of our being, connecting head with heart. Through these processes, we can bring about a more just and peaceful world.

4

—

Re-envisioning Education

Western universities regard objectivity as neutral, and subjectivity as biased. Education needs to be re-envisioned to include the cultivation of wisdom, as well as learning to live in society and overcoming oppression and exploitation. This broader view of education waned in the eighteenth century during the Age of Enlightenment, when the brain and individualism overtook sensibility and cooperation.

Buddhist education begins with humanity's ultimate questions: What is the meaning of life? What is our own deepest nature? What is our responsibility to others? Buddhism does not separate life from education. Nalanda—the world's first university—was founded in the second century in India, and became a flourishing center of Buddhist and academic studies. Nalanda had a vast library and a faculty of leading scholars and Buddhist practitioners. According to accounts of Chinese pilgrims who visited there, 10,000 monks from all over Asia were studying logic, medicine, mathematics, and Buddhism. Nalanda University lasted for a thousand years.

Today's universities, according to eco-scholar Thomas Berry, are "the most dangerous institutions in the world." They produce armies of economic rationalists who march away from real problems. Pursuing "value-neutral" science, they overlook genuine moral and spiritual issues, and are deeply implicated in a global economy that puts rationality at the service of financial interests while subverting efforts at personal and political integration. Despite the smokescreen of philanthropy for the humanities and liberal arts, big money for big science is big business. Berry has proposed that universities appoint deans of morality to ensure that questions of value be taken seriously.

In the nineteenth century, political leaders subordinated faith and culture to science, economics, sociology, anthropology, philosophy, and history. Scientism, the dogmatic application of the scientific method to all fields of knowledge, believes that only the rational mind is sufficient to observe and understand reality. It focuses exclusively on the material and quantitative, demeaning the spiritual and qualitative. What isn't rational is regarded as outside the scope of scientific inquiry and therefore of little value.

Thanks to mainstream science, our knowledge about the universe has expanded exponentially, and we have gained control over malevolent natural phenomena and learned to cure many diseases. But at what cost? Alongside electricity, transportation, communications, and medical care, we see devastated landscapes, squandered resources, reduced biodiversity, and an increase in the numbers of weapons of mass destruction. Science and technology divorced from human values and ethical accountability are easily swayed by greed and often insensitive to the moral laws of cause and effect.

In the years ahead, corporate control of both human and nonhuman life will broaden and deepen. Corporations are altering the genetic structure of plants and animals and claiming ownership and patent rights to these modified life forms. Local producers—including indigenous people and other farmers—are losing the right to grow crops their ancestors planted for millennia. The Global Biodiversity Treaty adopted in 1992 at the Rio Earth Summit may, paradoxically, further encourage these trends, creating a framework by which global interests can continue to draw on the developing world's biodiversity. We must be wary of green capitalism, which projects an illusion of environmentalism, while seeking to exploit and manage the resources of poorer nations and peoples.

In the post-Cold War world, capitalist triumphalism has bred hubris and delusion. Free-market capitalism preached by the neoliberal school of economics is a stark manifestation of this. Tolerance for socioeconomic diversity and alternative models of development is still almost nonexistent. Formerly diverse ways of life worldwide continue to be eroded by consumerism and the implementation of neoliberal policies.

Present-day education has become too parochial. We obtain a degree merely to find a high-paying job. Rarely is any voice heard from below, from the margins. It is really a system of imposed ignorance, reinforcing the internalized power structures and immunizing us against self-understanding. For education to be more effective, it has to be dialogical, inclusive, and compassionate, and needs to heal the rift between body and mind. Buddhist practice addresses these issues through the cultivation of mindfulness, which includes meditation and precepts, which are guidelines for living a moral life.

Rural people understand the wholeness of life and the sanctity of the natural order. They can teach us to stay attuned to nature and to live in balance with dignity and a sense of the sacred. We need to balance the advances of science with the wisdom of indigeneity. We need education that encourages us to integrate the many aspects of our being. Through meditation and art, we can connect with our mother earth and reaffirm our cooperative nature, recognizing the environment as part of ourselves. Planting seeds of peace, turning inward toward ourselves, we can heal ourselves and heal our planet. Richard Rodriguez writes, "Education requires radical self-reformation."

In the West, education is viewed as a means of gaining knowledge skills or other forms of human capital that will assist us in earning a living. As an alternative, Adam Curle suggests, "Education is a learning process that pulls out the hidden potentials in each person, that facilitates self-creation through self-realization." This is similar to Buddhist education.

Buddhist pedagogy does not separate education from life. For Buddhists, the objective of education is liberation from ignorance. The

Buddha taught the threefold training (*tisikkha*)—wisdom (*pañña*), ethics (*sila*), and concentration (*samadhi*). Wisdom is the recognition of the interdependence of things. True wisdom is to understand the nature of reality without prejudice or attachments, seeing things as they are. When attained, this understanding blends with compassion, and helping others becomes an endless personal mission.

In Buddhist education, our intellect and emotions develop concurrently, and the praxis must be in congruence with society, facilitating an understanding of life and the world that is not marred by prejudice or selfishness. Buddhist education fosters a culture of peace by subduing the rising tide of insecurity, structural violence, and terror through compassion, humility, generosity, mindfulness, and wisdom.

We need cognitive diversity. Different forms of knowledge—equally valid—are needed for different circumstances. One type of knowledge is needed to get men to the moon, another to foster environmental sustainability. Certain forms of knowledge are needed to build super-bombs; other forms are needed to make peace. If modern medicine cannot heal my backache, I might go to an acupuncturist. This is common sense, and many examples can be drawn from daily life.

We uncritically accept "established knowledge." When our doctor fails to cure us, we rarely question his authority or that of his medical modality. Rather, we question our own knowledge, thinking we know less than this so-called expert. Modern education is the same. It posits an ignorant learner and a brilliant body of established knowledge conveyed unerringly by our professor. It is time for us to question the fundamentals of the Enlightenment in order to become truly enlightened.

The job of a university is not teaching as such, especially teaching students to be a special, privileged class. Giving lessons and training students—developing a basic foundation—should be the task of primary and secondary schools. At the university level, *learning* should be the priority. The university should be a place to explore and to learn. In the past, Thai education, with Buddhism as a core component, helped educate the people in ways to achieve happiness in their lives. Education became the art of cultivating happiness through perseverance, friendship, balance, and faith.

To *reform* means to change or destroy an old form. At no other time in history has education reform been so important for learning ways to meet our social and political challenges.

Art, music, and dance have always been part of my country's pedagogy, hospitality, and even diplomacy. Every time an official representative from Bangkok visited Chiang Mai, for example, the northern host would dance to welcome and entertain his guest. The southerner would dance along, and they'd enter the city together.

While farmers and peasants were weaving the cloth used to make their clothes, family members and coworkers would sing or play musical instruments to encourage them. People also sang while tilling the land or harvesting their crops; then they shared the harvest with neighbors and monks. Beauty was interwoven into the lifestyle, reflecting the rhythm of the seasons.

Today, we Thais have become estranged from a life this meaningful. Modernity has uprooted our traditional ways, and shopping malls have replaced temples as the centers of communal life. The upper and middle classes indulge in consumerism, depleting resources and polluting nature. Higher education produces servants of the powers-that-be, not compassionate, responsible citizens. The center of power has shifted from the Dharma to the Central Bank, a rich men's club that serves as the gatekeeper for multinational corporations.

The term *civilization* originally referred to urban life. Tagore observed that the culture of Asia is derived from the jungle, while the culture of the West is urban. Aristotle called city living the only way to cultivate beauty, goodness, and truth, because in the forest, you don't have time for these "luxuries." Rousseau believed that science and art are garlands that conceal the chains that bind and enslave us, and stifle "the sense of original liberty for which we have been born."

When we treat life as art and cultivate our own inner beauty and moral courage, it is palpable in the architecture, literature, and culture. The Assembly of the Poor, a living, participatory, self-organized movement, has called for a comprehensive reevaluation of the concept of beauty as a way to rediscover their cultural roots. The Assembly has linked up with an ad hoc educational institution called Midnight University. Based on local wisdom and culture combined with lessons on sustainability, conflict resolution, Buddhism, resource management, and networking, the Midnight University seeks to foster pride in a simple and beautiful way of life. It is the kind of education the people need to lead a prosperous life, nourishing hope and helping reduce exploitation and oppression. We can incorporate traditional concepts of beauty into our nonviolent struggles for justice, human rights, and the environment. To do so is to open another door to truth.

In his classic work on Buddhist economics, *Small Is Beautiful: Economics as if People Mattered*, E. F. Schumacher reminds us that human beings are incalculably more important than profits. He encourages us to return to right livelihood and appropriate technology, based on the teachings of the Buddha. By putting the human dimension back into economics, Schumacher offers a significant contribution to the alternative education movement.

Other Western thinkers, such as Ivan Illich, Paolo Freire, and Catholic theologians in Latin America, have challenged the Western worldview from a Western standpoint, based on logic and science. As Illich put it, schooling is modernity's rite of passage, the "central myth-making ritual of industrial societies." Schools ensure the pupils' "full commitment to the ideology which puts economic growth first," while the university becomes the "final stage of the most all-encompassing initiation rite the world has ever known." Language becomes so perfectly attuned to the agendas of the powerful that the concepts and connotations with which resistance could be formulated are eliminated, making protest appear irrational and naïve. Students are not taught critical thinking, but to freeze the present. Reason is assumed to be neutral, and intuition, transcendence, and mystery are invisible in this one-dimensional discourse.

In this consumerist monoculture, individuals are alienated from their natures, their cultures, and one another. Empowerment education for grassroots communities provides tools to counteract these trends. Education needs to address our outer *and* inner landscapes. We need to go beyond science and find alternative technologies to help us realize peace and freedom within, and use these technologies to engage with society to benefit all. We must chart the roots and the *routes* of our cultures and their interconnections. We cannot return to the past, but we can retrace the past with an open mind to create a science that is morally inclined.

Societies would be healthier if they advanced sustainability rather than unlimited growth, if they were places where people would help one another in hard times, where power would be shared rather than fought over, where nature would be revered rather than exploited, where spirituality and wisdom would be honored. There are committed people worldwide working to manifest this vision. With clear awareness of the structural violence in society and within themselves, they are on the path of a bodhisattva, working for the liberation of all. This challenging yet enriching path of education is a combination of contemplation and activism, spirituality and politics, humor and seriousness. In Asia, engaged young people are using jewels of their Buddhist tradition to guide their efforts to create a sustainable future.

❖❖❖

For human beings to live happily, we must have physical, social, and inner freedom. Physical freedom—the freedom to live in harmony with nature and the environment—includes freedom from want and deprivation; an adequate supply of food, clothing, shelter, and medicine; and the ability to deal with natural dangers when they arise. Social freedom—freedom in relationship with fellow humans—allows us to live together safely without being exploited. Inner freedom allows us to live independently, content within, not needing to exploit nature or our fellow humans.

In the West, the predominant approach to curing social ills is through social engineering. In Buddhist countries, we work to integrate our heads and hearts and address these problems in an integrated fashion. After understanding the first noble truth of suffering, we must examine the causes of our suffering.

As third-world countries jump on the consumer bandwagon, our educational systems become second-class copies of Western education and produce shortsighted, self-centered ideas, sometimes even appropriated from our own traditions and indigenous wisdom. We need to rediscover forms of cultural resistance and inspiration in our own traditions to withstand the destructive march of consumerism and techno-capitalism. We need to create forums for local people in the face of globalization's threats to our cultures and economic integrity. We need to offer a spiritually based, ecologically sound, holistic education to increase confidence in our heritages and find ways to resist structural violence.

I have worked for many years to create a Center for Sustainable Communities, whose mission is to nurture spiritually and culturally appropriate development models based on a holistic understanding of development. This includes promoting values common to all religious and spiritual traditions, empowering participatory civil society, preserving indigenous and ethnic wisdom, and encouraging an ecological worldview. This center will be a demonstration, research, and training institute in small-scale appropriate technologies, sustainable forestry and agriculture, ecological economics, management skills, and small-scale, income-generating activities. It will provide training in new development projects and the rehabilitation of degraded communities and ecosystems and integrate the spiritual, cultural, ecological, and technological aspects of sustainable development with the purpose of empowering grassroots communities.

This idea has grown out of collaboration among grassroots NGOs that have been working together for decades, conducting appropriate education and residential training programs under the banner of the Spirit in Education Movement (SEM). We have held courses in alternative development, deep ecology, conflict resolution, nonviolent action, Buddhist economics, alternative politics, art, emerging holistic worldviews, globalization and its impact, and meditation for social action.

In 1996, SEM created a curriculum for a three-month grassroots training for religious leaders from ethnic minority groups in Asia. The program had three components: (1) perspective development, (2) exposure to grassroots initiatives, and (3) management-skills training. Many participants then went back to their countries and started small-scale, community-development projects with a participatory, bottom-up approach based on their spiritual beliefs. We now conduct this course annually, with follow-up programs in each participating country.

In 1997, SEM began a similar training course for second-rank leaders from the Assembly of the Poor in Siam. These people had been negatively affected by development projects run by government and big businesses. Many had been relocated as a result of dam construction. This course was intended to empower these poor farmers to start appropriate-development projects that are sustainable and affirm their cultural values.

This work resulted in an Alternatives to Consumerism Conference that brought 200 spiritual, NGO, and community leaders together to discuss participatory and appropriate-scale development that would alleviate poverty without stimulating overconsumption. A network of seventy people is now actively engaged in identifying and documenting alternative cultural models and developing curricula for use at the village level. From this work, we have identified the need for a broader curriculum within the residential training at the proposed Center for Sustainable Development. The center will serve as a base for grassroots leadership training in our region.

Throughout the third world, despite decades of so-called development, many poor, marginalized, and minority communities are still struggling for survival, cultural identity, and autonomy. Younger leaders from these communities need to understand the state of the world, obtain practical skills that will be useful in participatory development activities, and get access to appropriate technology and small, sustainable, income-generating activities. Once equipped in this way, they will become invaluable assets for their communities to mobilize local resources to alleviate poverty, as well as build up an immune system to protect them from the destructive aspects of modernization.

The lessons we've learned from the NGO movement confirm that this aim is viable. We only need to tap into our rich experiences. Communities tackling burning issues are working out possible solutions to problems like food insecurity, lack of education, hand-to-mouth living, and debt. Projects like credit unions, community income-generating activities, sustainable agriculture, and leadership training are underway and have become self-sufficient. Participants include Christian ministers, whose experiences in Siam and the Philippines have become the basis for lively sermons that question the dominant development model and promote community and appropriate-scale enterprises.

The Center for Sustainable Communities will have a spiritual base in its teaching and will welcome people from all faiths. All programs aspire to be culturally relevant to the diverse ethnic groups and tribal cultures and are participatory in all aspects, with gender awareness and sensitivity. Technologies are culturally appropriate and, wherever possible, made with locally available elements. All programs will be grassroots-oriented to help build civil society by empowering leadership from the bottom up. Ecologically sustainable lifestyles and programs to restore and rehabilitate what has been destroyed will be encouraged through teaching community-development skills and environmental-restoration techniques and practices.

The specific objectives of these training programs are:

- To enhance the capacity and effectiveness of grassroots leadership by strengthening a spiritual base and clarifying local values of community organizers and activists.
- To offer grassroots leadership training to the poor, the marginalized, and the minorities to build their capacity to help their communities survive and retain their cultural identity and autonomy.
- To create a demonstration center in small community-development activities with organic agriculture and appropriate technology.
- To use a bottom up, culturally appropriate approach in all activities.

A plan of action has been developed:

- These programs will serve spiritual leaders who come to relate development to their cultural traditions; grassroots NGO leaders and community organizers who are struggling to find appropriate development models for their communities; and village leaders striving to keep their traditional self-reliant way of life.

- The courses offered will draw from several broad areas of alternative education such as spirituality, holistic worldview, community skills development, and sustainable development in agricultural and small-scale business methods.
- The participants' connection with their own spirituality will be enhanced through forest walks, meditation, yoga, and other contemplative practices.
- Healthy communities are necessary for conflicts to be resolved, and consensus in decision-making can help people lead happier lives and avoid being so vulnerable to deception by promises made by big business in regard to development projects in rural and remote areas.
- Finally, sustainable technology that can improve the prosperity of communities and nations without depleting the land or sapping the people's spirits. Some examples are slope agriculture, biointensive agriculture, composting, food storage and preservation, sustainable forestry, well drilling, and small-scale sanitation and water treatment systems.

Education that is both practical and contemplative is at the heart of peacebuilding.

5

—

MORAL GOVERNANCE

Politics is about finding and maintaining consensus. People will always have difficulties with the way things are. Good politics needs to allow for vigorous debate and even dissent and resistance. Politics today has become confused with technocratic enabling— providing military security and economic stability for those in power.

Moral governance nurtures a fundamentally egalitarian relationship between the governor and the governed. At its best, it is like the relationship of spiritual friends. Without the give and take of real politics, governance becomes unreflective and, consequently, oppressive. Leaders who claim to be fighting terrorism often present themselves as on the side of good, and they use this to disregard the human costs of their wars, vis-à-vis both the terrorists and those at home. Uncontrolled development is another example of mindless governance, without regard for environmental protection or individual happiness.

When a leader tells the governed that there are no alternatives, politics is dead. "There are no alternatives" because the people don't have the will to look squarely at the situation and take action. As long as they think only about their own comfort and material well-being, there will be no alternatives. But when the people take the time to reflect, politics always has a seat at the table. Democracies have safeguards such as one person, one vote; separation of powers; checks and balances; and the rule of law that must not be forgotten.

If a leader is virtuous, the people will look to him as a role model. If the courts or legislatures mete out punishments that are too severe or arising from prejudice, the government will fail. The same applies if they are too lenient. In the exercise of power, the legislature, the courts, and the country's leader must be just and impartial, and uphold moral values. If anyone fails to do so, they must be removed from power.

When the Buddha delivered his first sermon, he set in motion the wheel of the Dharma, initiating the rule of righteousness for the welfare and happiness of the many. In a Buddhist democracy, the leader's responsibility is to protect the principles of Dharma and urge his fellow citizens to do the same. The Buddha himself created a democratic constitution for his monastic community. At its foundation was the understanding that people matter.

Buddhist community laws—*vinaya*—are thus democratic, with the reasons for the enactment of each law stated clearly. In general terms, they are:

1. For the welfare of the community
2. For the convenience of the community

3. To curb miscreants
4. For the ease of well-behaved monks
5. To restrain misbehavior in the present
6. To check future misbehavior
7. To help those who have faith to acquire more faith
8. To help those who have faith be strengthened in their faith
9. To help the good doctrine last long
10. For the promotion of discipline

Buddhist democratic law is based on mindfulness training and is the ethical basis that gives its followers direction. We respect the law when we see it work. Those who transgress are disciplined. Those who obey find that their faith in life is easy. The norm confers power to the law. The Buddha asked his followers to treat the Dharma and vinaya as their teachers.

In Buddhist democracies, the rule of law is consistent in statement and application. Buddhist laws respond to actual experience and are not imposed as though divinely ordained. Each party must be listened to and their arguments considered and evaluated fairly. Ill-will must not color a leader's judgment. In the *Mahavastu*, it is stated, "When a dispute arises, a ruler should pay equal attention to both parties and hear the arguments of each and decide according to what is right. He should not act out of prejudice, hatred, ignorance, or fear."

The Buddha is the archetypal embodiment of wisdom and fairness. In Buddhist political theory, the people are responsible for the quality of their leaders. When a leader is not righteous, he forfeits his right to lead. His misrule is considered the result of people choosing the wrong leader. He is neither above nor immune to the law. He is answerable in the same way as an ordinary citizen. The idea that a leader can do no wrong is alien to Buddhist thinking. Buddhist teachings regard every individual equal and responsible for the volitional acts he commits. The law of karma applies to everyone, regardless of class. No leader can claim special powers or immunity to laws to which everyone else is subject.

Buddhist teachings emphasize self-reliance, personal effort, and taking responsibility. The purpose of life in Buddhism is to attain freedom, happiness, and knowledge. Thus, the laws should not hinder personal development, but should foster actions that lead to the happiness and welfare of all.

The justice system adopted for the community of monks begins by treating everyone equally. Judges are selected carefully, based on their character, wisdom, experience, impartiality, and appreciation of the rules of righteousness. Complaints have to be brought without malice and with compassion for the accused, who is presumed neither guilty nor innocent. The accused must be willing to abide by the verdict.

The court recreates the crime scene, making the accused participate in it, to help him realize the social, physical, psychological, and spiritual dimensions of the alleged violation. Then a wise and experienced monk presents the essential background and implications of the charges on the basis of law and morality. He is not there as a prosecutor, but to help the court understand the accused and view the offense with compassion. The accused then examines the evidence presented and introduces further evidence and considerations, if he wishes.

Buddhist secular law and judicial systems have been constructed so that every opportunity is provided for the accused to prove his innocence. In successive trials, from the lowest to the highest courts, he is discharged if innocent and tried again in a higher court if found guilty. The process is designed to convince him that every possible opportunity has been offered and he has no grounds to complain. When judgment is rendered, traditional law books are consulted and punishment meted out accordingly. Rehabilitation involves not only the accused, but also the community. This makes it possible for him, after rehabilitation, to re-enter a rehabilitated community. Buddhist discipline is based on restorative justice and rehabilitation, not retribution. Their belief in karma led them to devise a system that avoids inflicting unjustified penalties. The law of karma affects the judge, also. He knows that if he is not impartial, he will suffer the karmic effects of his actions.

The most serious punishment is expulsion from the Sangha. That happens when a monk indulges in one of the four serious crimes, *parajikas*: (1) engaging in sexual activity (the Sangha is a community of celibate monks and nuns), (2) stealing, (3) killing, and (4) claiming to have spiritual powers that he does not have. The punishment for all other crimes ranges from probation to rehabilitation.

The judicial system of any democratic country can be run on a similar basis. The belief in the possibility of transforming human nature, the need to approach the wrongdoer with mercy and understanding, and the doctrine that officials are responsible (on the basis of their karma) for the work they do, even in official capacities, leads to a reformatory theory of jurisprudence.

The art of moral governance in Siam is derived from Brahmanism. King Rama I (1782–1809) ordered a mural of the Hindu classic work, *The Ramayana,* be painted at the Temple of the Emerald Buddha to reaffirm his commitment to this form of justice. Rama serves as a role model, and all the kings of the Chakri dynasty are thus named Rama. Reflecting on *The Ramayana,* Rama I compared his subjects to weapons more powerful than the kingdom itself. The kingdom is an organic body—the king is the heart and the people are the rest of the body. If they do not exist in harmony, the kingdom will perish.

In secular Buddhist societies, the assembly of monastics advises the state how to use power wisely and justly. If the Sangha upholds morality while staying knowledgeable about world affairs, it serves its role to check the power of the party in power. The Thai triad of Nation, Religion, and King was invented during the reign of Rama VI (1910–1925), based on the British slogan of God, King, and Country. Elevating the role of religion in this way does not mean that one religion is the best. Buddhadasa Bhikkhu cautioned that we not be carried away by any ism—nationalism, militarism, capitalism, or Buddhism. We must understand and respect others' religions as well as those who don't believe in religion. To overcome life's challenges, it is essential that we all cooperate. Good governance in a Buddhist democracy relies on compassion and nonviolence, emphasizing our shared humanity and the interdependence of all sentient beings. Nonviolence affirms our common vulnerability. We rely on the kindness of strangers.

Rulers must be sincere and humble, willing to learn from people of every walk of life, not just from technocrats, businessmen, and the privileged. We must interact with one another if we are to find and address the root causes of suffering. The governor and the state are not the same. A constitution must be a check on state power. Each branch must be accountable. "The King is dead, long live the King." When seen as a symbol, a force for national unity, the individual in power must not confuse his person with his role. He must act as an umbrella for the people.

When good governance erodes, one or more of the three poisons of greed, hatred, and ignorance is always present. The abuse of power represents hatred, and the excessive accumulation of wealth represents greed. If greed takes root in an administration, the institution will become mired in the quicksand of consumerism and highly vulnerable to manipulations by lobbyists and other politicians. Thai King Rama V wisely instructed his first crown prince, "A good monarch should be poor and love the people more than himself." Worse than greed and hatred is ignorance. The leader must act in an enlightened manner, illuminating the way to holistic understanding, while allowing dissent and criticism. For this to happen, the leader must not be beyond reproach or criticism. Criticism helps narrow privilege and cultivate accountability.

For morality to grow and become the normal state of affairs, the leader and the constitution must nurture one another. A good leader can awaken us from injustice. In an age of imperialism, capitalism, and terrorism, in a globalizing world, if we know how to transform leadership into a morally courageous institution, we won't have to kowtow to illegitimate or ignorant forces. Leadership can be one of our bulwarks, along with the constitution, and can act as a wheel of Dharma guiding the nation away from exploitation. The Sangha must rely on the Dharma-Vinaya for its constitution, and cooperate with courageous citizens to guide the nation away from greed, hatred, and ignorance.

All democracies must be mindful of the ethical norms needed in the contemporary world and treat their people as though *they* are the rulers. When leaders are arrogant, recalcitrant, working too closely with the military, standing above other citizens, or disdaining progressive individuals, their power will only obstruct change and jeopardize their own viability.

His Majesty Jigme Singye Wangchuck, the former King of Bhutan, declared that the ultimate purpose of government is to promote the happiness of the people. He said that Gross National Happiness (GNH) is more important than Gross National Product. This is a promising new path, worth exploring. We need a concerted effort of scientists, economists, spiritual practitioners, and government leaders to operationalize it, to develop the kinds of yardsticks we need to judge human progress and human happiness.

A key question facing Bhutan is: What happiness does the government seek to measure? For simplicity's sake, let us think of short-term happiness as being obtained chiefly through material goods, while spiritual, cultural, and social experiences promote a longer-term happiness.

Both elements—short and long-term, material and spiritual—are part of what brings us happiness. The question is one of balancing material needs with spiritual, cultural, and social needs. Satisfying the latter is very personal. Even if the government plays a role in these areas, like building theaters or funding the arts, fulfillment will vary from person to person.

Internationally recognized happiness surveys have been conducted by *New Scientist* magazine, the University of Michigan, and others. Critics of these surveys argue that they are too simplistic and fail to capture important aspects that would be integral to understanding public happiness. The *New Scientist* study concluded that Nigerians are the happiest people on earth, followed by Mexicans. Venezuelans. Russians, Armenians, and Romanians were rated the least happy. The United States was sixteenth. Money seems to play at least a partial role in creating happiness, but certainly is not the only factor. This has been corroborated by other studies.

Should Bhutan pay attention to how the happiness of its people rates in comparative global surveys? Or should the government pay attention only to whether its people are happy or not, regardless of its international happiness ranking? Getting caught up in global happiness rankings might be a misguided effort to "keep up with the Joneses." A Buddhist approach would place greater emphasis on subjective happiness, without comparison to others.

Finding ways to quantify Gross National Happiness would help states know whether their GNH is increasing or decreasing. However, if the GNH in a given year increases by such and such a percent, what does that mean? It seems most important simply to know whether people are happy or not.

Here are some potential indicators of happiness:

- the degree of trust, social capital, cultural continuity, and social solidarity
- the general level of spiritual development and emotional intelligence
- the degree to which basic needs are satisfied
- access to and the ability to benefit from health care and education
- the level of environmental integrity, including species loss or gain, pollution, and environmental degradation

The degree to which basic needs are satisfied is easy to measure—access to basic health care, education, and safe drinking water, for example. But measuring more superficial needs that also contribute to happiness is more difficult.

Left unimpeded, nature works in essentially a fundamentally cooperative way. We humans could organize ourselves on the same basis, recognizing that we are part of the natural order and not the dominant agent. Cultivating this kind of cooperative spirit and living close to nature can be the basis for a good life. The environment has long been a priority in Bhutan. Sixty percent of the country is protected forest, and another 26 percent is protected land. Given this commitment to the environment, it makes sense to include a measure of environmental integrity in calculating GNH. The percentage of protected land might be a starting point, but ways should also be found to measure the loss of environmental quality, such as pollution levels and the rate of species extinction.

Currently, GNH in Bhutan is an ideal, something to live up to, rather than something being measured precisely. Once GNH is successfully operationalized in Bhutan, I suspect that other countries will follow. The key, of course, is to create indicators that become instruments of liberation.

I am a radical conservative. I believe in justice, people power, and the value of a highly visible and righteous leader. The duty of any leader is well-captured in this verse from the Buddhist scriptures:

> When kings are righteous, the ministers of kings are righteous. When ministers are righteous, householders are righteous. This being so, the moon and the sun, constellations and stars go properly in their course. Days and nights, months and fortnights, seasons and years proceed, winds blow as they must. When crops ripen, men are long-lived, strong, and free from illness.

6

—

Real Security

Restructuring political and economic institutions cannot, in themselves, bring about liberation. Personal transformation is the starting place. Peace can prevail in a society only when individuals in that society are at peace. When greed, hatred, and ignorance govern our personal affairs, they will also be present in our society's institutions, preventing lasting social change. Real security depends on working on ourselves.

I am not suggesting that we focus only on inner work to the exclusion of social activism. When we accept systems that allow misconduct, we implicitly affirm that behavior as acceptable. Personal and social liberation are two sides of the same coin. We work on ourselves *while* we confront oppressive social systems. If we do this, when we encounter resistance or even retaliation from those who want to maintain the status quo, our mindfulness will help us gauge the danger, avoid trouble, and forgive our enemies.

When Daw Aung San Suu Kyi's political party, the National League for Democracy, won a landslide victory in Burma in 1990, the military junta refused to transfer power to them. Instead, they placed Aung San

Suu Kyi under house arrest and brutally cracked down on her supporters. In *Freedom from Fear*, she explains how she has fought nonviolently against the dictators since then—by meditating daily on loving kindness and extending compassion to the oppressed *and* the oppressors.

Some years ago, I participated in a march past the World Bank headquarters, to the Chinese Embassy in Washington, D.C., to protest a plan to build a giant dam in Tibet. China was seeking the World Bank's financial support for the project. Because of our demonstration, we were able to persuade the Bank not to support this project, whose social and environmental impacts would have been devastating. One of my fellow demonstrators, a Tibetan monk in his seventies, told me that he'd been imprisoned and tortured by the Chinese for eighteen years. After being released, he escaped to India and met with His Holiness the Dalai Lama. The Dalai Lama asked whether he had been afraid, and he replied that he was never afraid of pain or death, but of losing compassion for his tormentors. He did not regard them as enemies, but as fellow human beings forced to carry out their duties.

The Dalai Lama is an inspiring model of someone opposing oppression while cultivating peace within. He has seen the profound suffering of his people under Chinese rule, yet he continues to live happily and simply. I am convinced that one day Tibet will be free from Chinese domination and that the moral courage of Aung San Suu Kyi will one day free the people of Burma.

Buddhist precepts are not commandments. They are practices of self-cultivation, unenforced obligations based on taking personal responsibility. There are no supernatural interventions, only a certain immanence in the Buddhist self, shaped by nature, culture, politics, and history. The basis of our shared humanity is interdependence. *Not-self* in Buddhism suggests a certain opacity in us. Ethics become possible when we realize that we are incomplete. Vulnerability is a precondition for ethical relationships. Through meditation, an agency arises in us no longer bent on predatory mastery but on hospitality. Trying to create a fortress, a gated community for the self, can never work. There is always a "we." Our only enemies—greed, hatred, and ignorance—are within us. External enemies are primarily projections of our inner fears. We rely on each other.

When we are having difficulty seeing through the lens of interdependence, the Buddha suggests that we focus on the four *immeasurables*—loving kindness, the wish for the happiness and well-being of all; compassion, the wish for all to be free from suffering; altruistic joy in the good fortune of others; and equanimity, recognizing every being as equal.

One quarter of the world's population lives in the industrial North and consumes over 60 percent of the world's food, 85 percent of its wood, and

70 percent of its energy. More than a billion people in the agricultural South live in absolute poverty, without access to the essentials needed for survival. Disparities between classes and gender in the North and South are increasing. Women and children are disproportionately among the poorest everywhere in the world.

Development is a modern form of colonialism. We accept words like *underdeveloped*, *developing*, and *developed* without realizing that were imposed by former colonizers. The newer term, *globalization*, is even worse. The division is no longer Europe versus Asia, but rich versus poor, North versus South. The North impacts the South through investment for profit—selling manufactured goods, military equipment and training. The South pays with its natural resources and cheap labor, producing agricultural products at prices disadvantageous to small, local farmers, who pay alarmingly high interest rates for essential credit. Southern countries lose their indigenous cultures and state sovereignty, and suffer from environmental degradation, poverty, hunger, disloca-tion, and the development of urban slums. Meanwhile, the gap between rich and poor increases.

The North does not fare all that well, either. Its people are addicted to consumerism, mass culture, and drugs. They suffer from pollution, environmental degradation, and the loss of fundamental values. Urban populations face increasing crime, homelessness, and poverty. Those who are employed suffer from overwork, as the already excessive power of corporations increases. Individuals lose their sense of meaning and peace.

The provisions of international human rights treaties must not be undermined by the opportunism of authoritarian governments, even those that claim to be democratic. Global development models claim to cherish life but, in fact, starve it of meaning. They speak of making people happy, while blocking pathways to real peace. The material benefits of modernization and Westernization are unfairly distributed. Industrial capitalism has been built upon the violence of conquest, bondage, and debt. Exploitation continues to take new forms, including lopsided trading, structural adjustment, and third-world indebtedness. These policies increase the gap between the industrialized North and exploited South.

Inequality and exploitation lead to conflict. Conflicts we regard as ethnic or religious are often class-based, rooted in the social structures of the global economic system. As social disparities increase, violent repression is required to control populations. The global economy has become increasingly militarized. The world's leading nations produce huge quantities of weapons which they sell to both rich and poor countries. The armaments industry manufactures the equivalent of four tons of explosives per year for each of the earth's inhabitants, and the five permanent members of the United Nations Security Council—the U.S., UK, France, Russia, and China—export more than 85 percent of the world's arms.

This proliferation of weapons has created an extremely volatile global situation. More and more regions of the world—from the Middle East to Central America to Africa, Southern Asia, and Eastern Europe—are losing even the semblance of order. As terrorism spreads across the world, disappearances, torture, rape, and killing become all too commonplace. Fearing for their jobs, their lives, and their families, people do not speak out. There is also a dramatic increase of violence in homes, streets, and schools of industrialized countries, much of it directed against immigrants and other minorities.

Technology and capital are inextricably linked. Technological advances determine capitalist competition and growth. The processes of mechanization and commoditization move forward simultaneously. Subsistence economies are undermined as local people are forced to produce for international markets rather than their own community's needs. Tropical forests and coral reefs are destroyed in the name of development. Agribusiness, industrial manufacturing, nuclear weaponry, and toxic dumping pollute soil, air, and water. The damming of rivers destroys ecosystems and the people who inhabit them, along with their cultures and traditional wisdom. By increasing alienation, distrust, and fear among people, modernization makes it easier for them to be manipulated and controlled. Techno-capitalism is, ultimately, illogical. It destroys the natural integration of planetary life and threatens our very survival.

Local people worldwide are reacting. Indigenous and tribal peoples are struggling against the damming of rivers. Farmers are mobilizing against biotechnology. Mothers and wives are protesting disappearances.

In my country, Buddhist monks are ordaining trees to preserve forests. The challenges facing humanity will not be solved by more technology, markets, or bureaucracies, but by wisdom and compassion.

For indigenous people, what is most important is to live with dignity and a sense of the sacred, in harmony with the earth, revering ancestors, respecting communities, and affirming their commitment to future generations. Hill tribes in Siam, the Roma in Europe, Native Americans, Australian Aborigines, the Maori in Aotearoa, and other indigenous peoples can teach us how to choose local wisdom over the monoculture of globalization.

We need to support the many movements worldwide that are working toward reliance on local culture and communities. We need to re-envision the way governments and financial institutions provide and evaluate economic aid projects, such the overreliance on quantitative frameworks. When we measure infant mortality, life expectancy, literacy, and consumption rates, it belies the diversity and complexity of the human condition and presupposes *unlimited growth,* the worldview of most people in the West, as well as third-world elites. For the rest of humanity, where community economies and barter prevail, growth is cyclical, not linear.

The Pak Moon communities in northeast Siam lived harmoniously with their rice fields, their fishing, and the Moon River, following Buddhism and their ancient culture, for centuries. They were self-reliant and dignified. Then the World Bank concluded that these communities met the criteria of being poor and marginalized, and helped fund the Thai government's construction of the Pak Moon Dam in order to help them and others. In the process, the Bank and the government destroyed the villagers' way of life.

The World Bank now acknowledges that constructing large dams can have destructive consequences and has gone out of its way to listen to people's grievances. The World Bank's staff has traveled worldwide, interviewed more than 60,000 poor people, and produced a two-volume book, *Voices of the Poor.*

Some Asian leaders say that human rights are a Western invention—so they can abuse their own people with a clear conscience. In fact, the idea of human rights was developed in the context of resistance to Western empires. Human rights are as Eastern as they are Western, as Southern as Northern. Elements of what we call human rights can be found in the teachings of the Buddha and in the work of Muslim intellectual Chandra Muzaffar.

In Buddhism, human rights mean cultivating "we" simultaneously with "I," with a view of interconnectedness based on compassion. Venerable U Rewata Dhamma explained:

> The depiction of rights as simply a Western invention fails to understand the relationship of rights to responsibilities and ethical norms. The central values of all societies are very much the same. All ethical systems encourage people to love one another, and discourage killing, violence,

and so on. The universality and inseparability of human rights may therefore be understood as reflecting the universality and inseparability of inter-responsibility emerging from Dhamma.

Two decades ago, some of us felt a need to create an organization to find an appropriate role for Buddhism in the modern world. I call it buddhism with a small b, not clinging to any particular culture, school, or country. A socially engaged Buddhist movement had begun with the intention of creating a Buddhist liberation movement in Asia and beyond. In 1989, the International Network of Engaged Buddhists was founded to carry out this task. The challenges for contemporary Asian Buddhists is to convey the teachings of the Buddha in a way appropriate for the twenty-first century. Many Buddhists are skilled in teaching inner peace, which is at the core of any effective peace movement.

The post-colonial world needs to learn how to be modern without becoming Western. Embracing modernity in the context of development often goes hand in hand with imperialism. As such, the threat of alienation looms over those who unequivocally adopt such modernism. For the bulk of humanity, which is neither Western nor Caucasian, this problem must be addressed.

The capitalist promise of emancipation through continuous economic growth and technological advance has proved impossible. No economy can grow larger forever. Technological advances are not infinite.

Capitalism presupposes ever-increasing wealth. In reality, economic growth brings with it increasing income disparities. Noam Chomsky reports that nearly 60 percent of African American youth in New York City lack economic and educational opportunity, have no access to even the most basic social services, and little sense of security. Their plight is not significantly different from the inhabitants of Bangladesh. The BBC reported that the living conditions of some poor children in London are comparable to those Dickens wrote about in the nineteenth century.

After World War II, under the Labor Party, Great Britain established a welfare state. Socialism was able to plant its roots on British soil because intellectuals, writers, academics, and activists went to the grassroots to experience the suffering of the poor and marginalized. Working as a united front, they were able to tame capitalism in the context of a socialism that was not totalitarian. Forty years later, Mrs. Thatcher dismantled much of this work.

Before 1988, when Burma opened itself up to global capitalism, its countryside was lush and pristine. Since then, its natural environment has deteriorated at an alarming rate. The military junta has not only destroyed the country's forests, but also slaughtered many inhabitants.

Though professing socialism, China, Vietnam, and the former Soviet Union actually practiced totalitarianism. The suffering of poor people in these countries was mitigated by welfare programs organized by the state and the Communist Party that, unfortunately, only addressed material concerns while, at the same time, robbed the people of the initiative to cultivate self-reliance. Their people, including party cadres, were forced to parrot socialist principles. When the grip of totalitarianism weakened, capitalism easily engulfed these countries.

Kerala, a state in southern India, on the other hand, has had a communist government for most of the past fifty years. Based on their GDP per capita, the inhabitants of Kerala would be categorized as poor. However, Kerala has virtually full employment. The majority of peasants there cultivate food crops primarily for household consumption, selling only the surplus. The state's social welfare program fully incorporates the poorest and most marginalized inhabitants. Despite its economic poverty, Kerala has a higher literacy rate than the U.S., and its local politics are highly democratic.

Ladakh is a small province in the Indian state of Jammu-Kashmir. Its inhabitants are mostly Buddhist, while Muslims dominate the political and economic affairs of Jammu-Kashmir. Although materially poor, the residents of Ladakh are prosperous, in accord with the criteria noted on page 83.

A sustainable vision of the future cannot be rooted in the capitalist myth of emancipation. The future must be built on traditional wisdom and culture. It will not be found in New York or London but in communities with grassroots movements in Siam, Ladakh, and Kerala.

The future of the world must include the spiritual perspective of interconnectedness, a world founded on the principles of peace, nonviolence, and justice for all beings. It rests in every human heart that yearns for true contentment. When we learn to be self-reliant, selfrespecting, proud of our culture, humble and simple, generous and ever mindful, we will be prosperous indeed. Once we restructure our consciousness to be less self-centered, we can restructure our societies to be free from oppression and exploitation as well. According to the Buddha, like-minded friends are the most important external element for emancipation. We need good friends to help us develop ourselves and encourage our societies in the direction of peace and justice.

We should never think that our tradition is the best. We need to study and respect all traditions and practices. With an open heart, we can learn from many schools and collaborate with friends from different traditions and religions, even agnostics and atheists. All humans are spiritual beings. If people everywhere respect each other, it would form a strong moral force to overcome greed, hatred, and ignorance.

True wisdom comes from the head *and* the heart. It helps us know our limits and generates loving kindness and compassion. When we tune into our own suffering and the suffering of others, when we breathe mindfully throughout the day, peace and happiness arise, and we can share this peace with others. This is the foundation of true security.

7

—

Buddhism in a World of Change

Since the end of World War II, the disparity between the haves and
have-nots of the world has grown. Beginning with the postwar Marshall Plan, there was a one-way flow of resources from the advanced to
the developing countries to promote the latter's development. But, over
time, the powerful nations came to resent the dominance of smaller
nations at the UN, and the Big Five now exercise their Security Council vetoes too often for the UN to function as anything resembling a
democratic forum.

The high hopes entertained in the 1950s and 1960s of massive transfer
of capital and technological know-how from North to South along the
lines of the Marshall Plan, which had proved so vital for European recov-
ery, did not materialize, and the enthusiasm surrounding the launching
of the first UN Development Decade dissipated. When economic forces
are left to themselves, they tend to increase inequality. Countries that
protect the weak and promote justice within their national borders
became half-hearted in their support for the establishment of an international order based on justice, freedom, tolerance, and compassion.

The solidarity of humankind as an axiom was superseded by nationalism and the Cold War.

Every day, tens of thousands people starve to death in a world that has an abundance of food. The global economic system profits the fortunate minority, while more and more people are pushed into poverty. Twenty percent of the world's population controls more than 80 percent of its wealth. For the few to enjoy their comforts, others are deprived of basic needs. The economic forces of globalization, led by the Northern countries, along with multinational corporations and institutions like the World Bank, the International Monetary Fund, and the World Trade Organization, not only sentence millions to poverty, they create breeding grounds for hatred, which gives rise to violence.

First-world leaders create structures like the World Bank and believe they are reasonable. For most of the world's people, these institutions have inherent prejudices. People need to have the right to pursue their own style of development. When we impose our worldview on others, even when we believe deeply that it is righteous, it is structural violence.

In February 2009, former chief economist of the World Bank Joseph Stiglitz told an interviewer, "The model that was behind much of the impetus for globalization was based on free, unfettered markets. That model—deregulation—has failed. That was the kind of thinking that led to the problems the United States is in today."

The teaching of the Buddha offers much to mitigate the world's suffering. For more than fifty years, I have helped found seed projects, each of which has a material and a spiritual dimension. These projects are informed by the four noble truths and demonstrate ways in which the application of wisdom to social conditions can generate justice, peace, and ecological balance.

On a political level, mindfulness can help in our work against consumerism, sexism, militarism, and the many other isms that undermine the integrity of life. It can be a tool to help us criticize positively and creatively our societies, nations, and even cultural and religious traditions. Rather than hate our oppressors, we can dismantle oppressive systems. Is the international economic system that demands unlimited growth inherently defective? From a Buddhist perspective, the answer is yes.

Prosperity, from the Buddhist viewpoint, is self-reliance, self-dignity, pride in one's culture, contentedness, generosity, and mindfulness. In Buddhism, income and wealth are not indicators of prosperity. Buddhism values a peaceful life in which one relates harmoniously to all sentient beings and the environment. The senses are not overindulged, and thought, speech, and action are not abused. Consumerism endangers the biosphere and strengthens multinational corporations that care more about profit than the well-being of people. We must be mindful of how to create and use wealth.

Equality does not mean sameness. Some people need more than others. A sick person, for example, requires more resources than a healthy person. Equality tends to denote a process by which the middle classes and the poor strive to be like the rich and powerful. But equality could also be attained if the rich were to live more simply and share some of their wealth.

In *Small Is Beautiful*, E. F. Schumacher says, "The keynote of Buddhist economics … is simplicity and nonviolence." He describes Buddhist economies as those in which people share power, respect nature, and help one another; and he recommends development that avoids gigantism, especially of machines that tend to control rather than serve us.

The West became separated from its roots the year Christopher Columbus claimed to discover America. Asserting superiority over peoples who had been living there for thousands of years, they began looking forward without ever looking back. This lack of rootedness encourages discovery, but also permits such anomalies as creating labor-saving devices and unemployment at the same time.

Walt Whitman said, "I am large. I contain multitudes." I am not just Thai. My father's ancestors came from China. My Buddhism comes from India and Sri Lanka. I went to university in Great Britain, taught in North America, and have friends all over the world. Each of these heritages is in me. The Buddha taught that friends are "the whole of the holy life." Good friends encourage and criticize us. People ask if I'm not wasting my time attending meetings all over the world. I use up a lot of fuel flying to and from conferences. I suffer the awful food they serve.

Sometimes we use too much paper, wasting trees. But the more we talk with people, including those in power, the more likely they will eventually listen. When I speak with the Archbishop of Canterbury or the president of the World Bank, things won't change overnight, but it is a good sign that they are willing to listen. In the Pali language, the word for loving kindness is *metta*, derived from the root word for "friend." Buddhist insight and compassion are based on friendship. Schumacher recommends we practice economics "as if people mattered."

The founder of Buddhism was prince of a small state in northern India, now Nepal. Anguished by the problems of life, suffering, and death, he spent six years attempting to shine light on these mysteries, and his insight was the result of this inner research. He became a doctor to cure the ills of humankind.

Buddhism enters the life of society through individuals who have attained the peace of the Buddha. These individuals exercise *nonaction,* which means their very being is filled with love. In addition to meditation masters who spend their lives in forests, some wisdomkeepers are active in the world. Phrakru Sakorn is such a spirit. His district, Samut Sakorn, near Bangkok, is often inundated with seawater and it is difficult to grow rice there. So Phrakru helped his parishioners, mostly poor, illiterate farmers, work together to build dikes, canals, and roads. Then he suggested they grow coconut trees. When they did so successfully, he advised them not to sell their coconuts because middlemen kept the price low, but to make coconut sugar in the traditional way. With the help of a nearby university, Phrakru received community-development assistance, and the people of his district began selling coconut sugar all over Siam. After that, he encouraged them to grow palm trees for building materials and to plant herbs for traditional medicine.

Political and economic awareness are related to individual acts. To drink Coca Cola or Pepsi Cola in Siam is not just to ingest junk food, but to support exploitative values. Through their advertising, Pepsi and Coke make the villagers feel ashamed to offer rainwater to drink; they feel they must offer us something in a bottle. And each bottle costs them a full day's earnings. When Dole Pineapple expanded into Siam, they acquired thousands of acres of land from our poor yet proud farmers. At first, the company offered an excellent price for the crops these farmers grew on land that was once theirs. Then the company lowered the price, and still later, the farmers became their employees. There are no labor unions in the countryside, and without the right to strike, they are at the company's mercy.

Asian elites educated in the West have been unable to look beyond establishment models of development. Perhaps they feel threatened by alternative models, for an egalitarian society might not have room for them. In any case, the dominant model is based on economic growth as measured by GNP and GDP, which is the opposite of Schumacher's appreciation of human scale.

This Think-Big strategy of development has convinced us that if we just get the economics right, the rest of life's pieces will fall into place. It has encouraged third-world countries to seek massive funding for enterprises that benefit only multinational corporations. It has led us to trust overseas experts and overlook, even scorn, indigenous solutions. It has despoiled the countryside, turning our beautiful lands into commercial tracts. It has accelerated the migration of country folk into cities, resulting in some of the most unlivable cities in the world. There is a strong need for change. It is time to put people first.

8

—

THE BREATH OF PEACE

We have more than enough programs, organizations, parties, and strategies, but we still put all our faith in the power of action alone, especially political action, to alleviate suffering and injustice. Activists and secular intellectuals tend to see all malevolence as being caused by others, or the system, without appreciating how these negative factors also operate within themselves. They approach global problems as though social engineering will solve them, that personal virtue will inevitably result from the radical restructuring of society.

The opposite view—that transforming society requires personal and spiritual change first, or at least simultaneously—has been accepted by religious adherents for millennia. Those who want to change society must understand the inner dimensions of change. Valuing the spiritual dimension gives voice to humanity's depth. All descriptions of religious experience come down to being less selfish.

As personal transformation is achieved, we acquire a greater sense of moral responsibility. Social change and spiritual considerations cannot be separated. Religion is at the heart of social change, and social change is the essence of religion.

We cannot overcome the limits of the individual self in a hermetically sealed environment. The four noble truths—suffering, the causes of suffering, the cessation of suffering, and the path to its cessation—can be skillfully applied to social activism. The teachings of the Buddha transcend individual salvation.

The Buddha described three root causes of evil—greed (*lobha*), hatred (*dosa*), and ignorance (*moha*). Understanding these helps us recognize the causes of suffering and hints at how suffering can be overcome. Today, the dominant form of greed is consumerism; we try to overcome the emptiness of our lives by increased consuming. We are at the mercy of advertisers, and, inevitably, we are exploited. The lust for power, a form of hatred, can lure us to defend unjust social systems. Ignorance is caused, first and foremost, by inadequate education. When students are trained only with the skills needed to become employees and when our children are exposed to values only through TV and computer games, ignorance prevails. We memorize and compartmentalize, and do not develop critical thinking.

Suffering can be mitigated by right understanding. Buddhist practices, beginning with mindful breathing, permeate my activism. Mindful breathing helps build up awareness, and with awareness we realize we cannot solve problems alone. Employing critical self-awareness, we see that we need friends for our actions to be effective. Sometimes we need to confront, sometimes we need to dialogue. If the Buddha had returned to his solitude—saying he regretted those people getting old and dying, but that he was sorry, there was nothing he could do to help—there would be no Buddhism. We have to meet individuals who work at the World Bank, multinational corporations, governments, and empires with empathy and compassion. Buddhism is not a religion of blind faith, but of practice and experience. We have to taste the truth for ourselves.

Aesthetic satisfaction goes hand in hand with activism—appreciating our artistic traditions and using culture and the arts to help us achieve social and political goals. Culture is not limited by national boundaries. We can appreciate the jewels of all traditions. Indigenous peoples know how to live simply and have time to enjoy themselves in community. We must find lifestyles that bring us happiness without causing harm to others or the environment.

I was privileged to work with the Venerable Maha Ghosananda in the Khmer refugee camps after the Americans abandoned Cambodia to the Khmer Rouge, and later to the Vietnamese. He was trying to establish peace among the rival factions. It was difficult, but his determination was unstoppable. He invited me to conduct reconciliation workshops among rival Khmer monks and laypeople.

Buddhist societies tend to view things in the long-term. In Siam, great tragedies hardly merit the blink of an eyelid. These attitudes are widespread in societies that believe in karma. This view strengthens patience and perspective. The essence of the Buddhist tradition is to overcome selfishness and transform greed into generosity, hatred into loving kindness, and ignorance into wisdom.

The root of the word *buddha* means "to be awake." When we are awakened to simplicity and humility and aware of the suffering engendered by greed, hatred, and ignorance, our consciousness is restructured. We become mindful about ourselves and others, and naturally try to restructure society. Restructuring individual consciousness and restructuring society are complementary activities, and both are desperately needed. The Sarvodaya Shramadana movement in Sri Lanka applies Buddhist principles to awaken people first individually, then at the village and national levels, so that eventually all humankind will be awakened to live as one, in self-reliance, using appropriate technology.

The Buddha was a simple and humble monk. His teachings provide a unique way of seeing the world, and, if properly understood and practiced, can lead us to a noble life. The Dalai Lama, also a simple monk, is guiding many of us with his compassion, wisdom, and skillfulness to create a hopeful future. The Buddha taught that the wheel of righteousness (*dhammacakka*) must control the wheel of power (*anacakka*), that the rich and powerful, especially the rulers, must have only one overriding concern, that of upholding the Dharma.

❖ ❖ ❖

If I were to go to the Buddha and ask for a simple formula to resolve our modern dilemmas, he might say: "I breathe, therefore I am." Breathing is the most important element in our lives and in the life of every living being. Without breathing, we die. Breathing goes on day and night, twenty-four hours a day, seven days a week.

I learned this "Breath of Peace" exercise from Thich Nhat Hanh, and I have been practicing it ever since:

Breathing in, I calm my body.
Breathing out, I smile.
Dwelling in the present moment,
I know this is a wonderful moment!

Breathing in, I know that I am breathing in.
Breathing out, I know that as my in-breath grows deep,
        my out-breath grows slow.
Breathing in, I feel calm.
Breathing out, I feel at ease.
As I inhale, I smile.
As I exhale, I release all accumulated pressures.
Breathing in, I know there is only the present moment.
Breathing out, I know it is a wonderful moment.

This technique, called *samatha bhavana,* helps us maintain calmness. Once we have mastered this simple exercise, we are ready to practice insight meditation (*vipassana bhavana*) to create a critical awareness of the self and to avoid taking ourselves too seriously. In this way, we become less and less selfish and begin to seek peace and justice, based on a real understanding of ourselves and the world. We are no longer ruled by our greed, hatred, and ignorance.

Let us meditate for world peace, social justice, and environmental balance, beginning with our own breathing: I breathe in calmly and breathe out mindfully. Once I have seeds of peace and happiness within me, I will reduce my selfish desires and reconstitute my consciousness. With less attachment to self, I will try to understand the structural violence in the world. Linking my heart with my head, I see the world holistically, as a sphere filled with living beings who are all related to me. I expand my understanding with love, to help build a more nonviolent world. I vow to live simply and offer myself to serve those who are oppressed. By the grace of the compassionate one, with the help of good friends, may I be a partner in alleviating the suffering of the world so it will become a wholesome place for all beings to dwell in harmony.

May all beings be happy.
May all beings be free from suffering.
May all beings dwell in peace.

Acknowledgments

I am grateful to the many friends and colleagues who hosted the lectures and published the articles that are in *The Wisdom of Sustainability*. Phairot Chachoenram kindly typed the manuscript; my old friend Nicholas Bennett improved the English and edited the manuscript for length; and Arnie Kotler of Koa Books gave the book its shape.

I am grateful for Arnie's friendship over many years. At Parallax Press, he published *Seeds of Peace: A Buddhist Vision for Renewing Society* (1992), my first book in the U.S., and it became my best seller and was translated into German, Italian, Dutch, Korean, Sinhala, and Bhasa Indonesia. After leaving Parallax, Arnie introduced me to the editors of Wisdom Publications, who published *Conflict, Culture, Change: Engaged Buddhism in a Globalizing World* (2005). Now he has started a new press and has agreed to publish this volume, in collaboration with Trasvin Jittidecharak of Silkworm Books in Chiang Mai, Siam.

Last, but not least, I would like to thank my wife, Nilchawee, who has been supporting me in my various activities for forty-four years, with love, care, patience, understanding, and forgiveness.

Sulak Sivaraksa
Bangkok, Siam
Makarakhom 2552 / January 2009

About the Author

SULAK SIVARAKSA, born in 1933, is a prominent and outspoken Thai intellectual and social critic. He is a, scholar, publisher, activist, founder of many organizations, and author of more than a hundred books and monographs in both Thai and English, including *Seeds of Peace: A Buddhist Vision for Renewing Society* and *Conflict, Culture, Change: Engaged Buddhism in a Globalizing World.*

Educated in England and Wales and in a Buddhist monastery in his native Siam, Sulak founded *Sangkhomsaat Paritat* (Social Science Review) in 1963, and it became his country's foremost intellectual magazine, addressing the most important political and social issues during a time of military dictatorship. His work editing *Sangkhomsaat Paritat* led him to become engaged with grassroots organizations, where he learned the importance of staying in touch with the poor. Beginning in the late 1960s, he participated in a number of service-oriented, rural development projects, in association with Buddhist monks and student activists.

During the 1970s, Sulak became the central figure in a number of non-governmental organizations in Siam, including the Komol Keemthong Foundation (named for a young teacher killed in 1971), the Pridi Banomyong Institute (named for the father of Thai democracy), the Slum Childcare Foundation, the Coordinating Group for Religion and Society, the Thai Inter-Religious Commission for Development, and Santi Pracha Dhamma Institute. Through his involvement with these organizations, Sulak began to develop indigenous, sustainable, and spiritual models for change. Since then he has expanded his work to regional and international levels. He cofounded the Asian Cultural Forum on Development, the International Network of Engaged Buddhists, and the Spirit in Education Movement.

In 1976, Siam experienced its bloodiest coup. Hundreds of students were killed and thousands were jailed. The military burned the entire stock of Sulak's bookshop and issued an order for his arrest. Sulak was forced into exile and remained outside the country for two years. During that time, he served as a visiting professor at the University of California, Berkeley; Cornell University; the University of Toronto; and throughout Europe; and was able to continue his activist work in the West.

In 1984, he was arrested in Bangkok on charges of criticizing the king *(lèse majesté)*, but international protests led to his release. In 1991, another warrant was issued for his arrest, and Sulak was forced into political exile once again. He returned to fight the case in the court in 1992 and won in 1995. At the end of 1995, he was awarded the Right Livelihood Award, known as Alternative Nobel Peace Prize.

Sulak Sivaraksa sees Buddhism as a questioning process—question everything including oneself, look deeply, and then act from that insight. He has been one of a handful of leaders worldwide working to revive the socially engaged aspects of spirituality. At the core of his work is the mission to build new leadership for change at all levels. Sulak offers a unique perspective on how to work for peaceful, sustainable social change using the principles and practices of Buddhism as a personal and political resource. He has demonstrated that a life of contemplation and a life of political action can illuminate, inform, and encourage each other, and in fact, in his view, both are essential if either is to change for the better. For information, news, and updates, visit www.sulak-sivaraksa.org

OTHER BOOKS BY SULAK SIVARAKSA

Buddhist Perception for Desirable Societies in the Future (editor)

A Buddhist Vision for Renewing Society

Conflict, Culture, Change: Engaged Buddhism in a Globalizing World

Global Healing: Essays and Interviews on Structural Violence, Social Development, and Spiritual Transformation

Loyalty Demands Dissent: Autobiography of an Engaged Buddhist

Modern Thai Monarchy and Cultural Politics

Powers That Be: Pridi Banomyong Through the Rise and Fall of Thai Democracy

Religion and Development

Search for Asian Cultural Integrity (editor)

Seeds of Peace: A Buddhist Vision for Renewing Society

Siam in Crisis

Siamese Resurgence: A Thai Voice on Asia in a World of Change

A Socially Engaged Buddhism

Trans Thai Buddhism & Envisioning Resistance

Rediscovering Spiritual Values: Alternative to Consumerism from a Siamese Buddhist Perspective

About the Editors

ARNOLD KOTLER is editor of Koa Books. He received an M.A. in political science from the University of California, Berkeley, and studied Buddhism at the San Francisco Zen Center and with Vietnamese monk Thich Nhat Hanh. He founded Parallax Press in the mid-1980s and directed the press until 1999. He lives in Hawai'i with his wife, Therese Fitzgerald.

NICHOLAS BENNETT spent forty years living and working in some of the poorest, most remote parts of the world—twenty-five of these working for the United Nations and the World Bank. Throughout his career, he concentrated on community and educational development, struggling to improve human rights, tackling corruption, and creating more human-centered development strategies, in order to offer hope and the chance to improve their lives to some of the most marginalized and exploited people in the world. He started his forty-year odyssey walking around West Africa with no money, and has since lived and worked for many years in each of four African and two Asian countries. He implemented a Gandhian development program in the far west of Nepal in an area stretching from three-to-ten days walk from the nearest road. Throughout these years, he has been accompanied by his wife and raised four children. He has published over 100 articles and a dozen books, including *Zigzag to Timbuktu* in 1963, and *All in the Cause of Duty* in 2006. He has an M.A. in Politics, Philosophy, and Economics from Oxford University.

koa books

Koa Books publishes works on personal transformation, social issues, and native cultures. Please visit www.koabooks.com for a full list of recent and forthcoming titles.

Koa Books
PO Box 822
Kihei, Hawai'i 96753
www.koabooks.com